The Alchemy of Conflict Transforming Arguments into Connection

David N Johnson

ISBN: 9798862484960

Cover design by: David N Johnson
Printed in the United States of America

1st edition 2023

Dedication

To my wife, my children, and to you my dear reader. We can all use a little less conflict and a whole lot more connection in our lives.

Contents

Preface

We've all been there. The dinner table that turns into a battlefield, the workplace meeting that devolves into a shouting match, the online forum that transforms into a cesspool of vitriol. Conflict is as universal as humanity itself. But what if I told you that every disagreement, every heated exchange, and even every awkward silence is an untapped reservoir of potential growth and deep connection?

For far too long, society has conditioned us to view conflict as something to be avoided or won. This book challenges that paradigm. It invites you to see every disagreement as an opportunity—a chance to understand and be understood, to challenge and be challenged, to grow and help others grow. In essence, this book is about turning the base metal of conflict into the gold of connection, much like alchemists of old believed they could transform lead into gold.

The Argument That Changed Everything

Several years ago, I found myself embroiled in a heated argument with a close friend. The topic? Inconsequential in retrospect, but in the moment, it felt like the most important issue in the world. Voices were raised, accusations flew, and before we knew it, our friendship was on the brink of collapse.

Then something extraordinary happened. Instead of throwing in the towel, we decided to try a different approach. We paused, took a deep breath, and committed to understanding each other's point of view. What started as a fierce argument transformed into one of the most enriching conversations of my life. By the end of it, not only was our friendship salvaged, but it had deepened in a way I never thought possible.

That transformative experience was a watershed moment for me. It made me realize the untapped potential that lies within every conflict, and it set me on a path to explore this fascinating terrain. This book is the culmination of that journey, and it's my sincere hope that it will guide you in transforming your own conflicts into opportunities for growth and connection.

What You Can Expect to Gain

This book aims to equip you with a new lens through which to view conflict. It's not just a set of theories or abstract principles; it's a practical guide filled with real-life examples, actionable tips, and interactive exercises. By the end of this journey, you won't just be a passive observer of conflicts; you'll be an active participant in transforming them.

A Toolkit for Life

Beyond a mere set of guidelines for navigating specific disagreements, this book serves as a toolkit for life. The skills you'll acquire here—active listening, empathic understanding, effective apologizing—are universally applicable, whether you're negotiating a business deal, mending a fractured friendship, or navigating complex family dynamics.

Your Path to Growth and Connection

This isn't just a book; it's an invitation to a journey. A journey from the rigid constraints of ego and prejudice to the liberating landscapes of empathy and understanding. A journey that doesn't promise to be easy, but one that guarantees richness and depth. By embracing the principles in this book, you're not just resolving conflicts; you're enriching your life and the lives of those around you.

Introduction

It was an unusually cold winter evening, the kind where the frost seems to seep into your bones. Curtis and I found ourselves huddled in a dimly lit coffee shop, the orange glow of pendant lights creating a warm but tense cocoon around us. The steam rising from our cups of hot cocoa serv ed as a misty barrier, almost as if it were trying to absorb the palpable tension between us.

Curtis and I had been friends since college, our bond forged over late-night study sessions and shared life milestones. But that evening, the emotional stakes were high. A topic we were both deeply passionate about had surfaced, and the weight of our history together made the impending argument feel like a powder keg ready to explode.

The issue at hand was social justice, a topic we both cared about but saw from vastly different angles. As the conversation unfolded, it became apparent that our viewpoints weren't just divergent; they were on a collision course. The lines of the wooden table between us seemed to deepen, as if etching battle lines into its surface.

Just when it felt like our friendship was teetering on the brink, Curtis did something unexpected. He paused, took a deep breath, and said, "You know what, let's try to understand each other rather than win this argument." It was a simple statement, yet it diffused the tension like a pin to a balloon. The atmosphere shifted palpably, making room for something new—genuine curiosity.

We spent the next hour not arguing, but exploring—each of us stepping into the other's shoes, trying to see the world from a different viewpoint. The result was nothing short of transformative. Not only did we reach a deeper understanding of the issue at hand, but our friendship also emerged stronger, fortified by a newfound respect for each other's perspectives.

By choosing constructive conversation over destructive argument, we both gained more than just a resolution to our disagreement. We

4

experienced a personal epiphany, a realization that our perspectives weren't fixed points but evolving landscapes shaped by the quality of our interactions. It was a lesson in the transformative power of dialogue, one that has stayed with me and inspired much of what you will read in the pages that follow.

The Importance of Constructive Conversations in Today's World

In a world awash with information yet starving for wisdom, the art of constructive conversation has never been more critical. The elephant in the room? Our social and political landscape is more polarized than ever. The divides are not just ideological but emotional, creating rifts in families, friendships, and communities. From social media echo chambers to increasingly contentious political debates, it's as if society has lost its shared language for disagreement. We are quick to label, to demonize, and to cancel, often forgetting that behind every viewpoint is a human being with their own set of experiences and values.

If you've picked up this book, it's likely that you've felt this tension in your own life. Perhaps you've sat across from a loved one, struggling to bridge an ideological chasm. Or maybe you've found yourself biting your tongue in a work meeting, fearful of the repercussions of speaking your mind. These are not just isolated incidents; they're symptoms of a larger societal ailment—one that makes the cultivation of constructive conversations both a rarity and a necessity.

The Power of Dialogue

If conflict is the spark, then dialogue is the crucible where transformation occurs. But what is genuine dialogue? It's far more than just an exchange of words or a volley of arguments. At its essence, dialogue is a shared exploration, a mutual journey into the complex terrain of human thought, emotion, and experience.

Through dialogue, we accomplish several things. First, we defuse tension. Dialogue creates a container for emotions, allowing them to be expressed without causing harm. It's the difference between a controlled burn and a wildfire—the former enriches the soil for new growth, while the latter devastates the landscape.

Second, dialogue fosters creativity. When we engage in constructive conversations, we're not just solving problems; we're discovering new possibilities. The interplay of diverse perspectives can lead to creative solutions that would be impossible to achieve in a confrontational setting.

Lastly, dialogue enriches us. It exposes us to viewpoints we may never have considered, challenging our preconceptions and widening our understanding. Through genuine engagement, we acquire not just tolerance but respect for the other, seeing them not as an opponent to defeat but as a partner in a shared quest for truth.

Personal and Societal Stakes

Mastering the art of constructive conversation isn't just a personal endeavor; it's a societal imperative. Think of it as the "butterfly effect" of communication. Each constructive conversation you have creates a ripple effect, impacting not just you and your immediate conversational partner, but also the networks to which you both belong.

On a personal level, the stakes are high. Your ability to engage in constructive conversation affects your relationships, your emotional well-being, and even your career prospects. It's a life skill, as essential as financial literacy or emotional intelligence.

But the stakes go even further. By fostering constructive conversations in your immediate circles, you contribute to a cultural shift. The more people engage in meaningful dialogue, the more it becomes the norm rather than the exception. This has a compounding effect, creating communities that value empathy, openness, and mutual respect. In a world where division seems to be the order of the day, the ability to converse constructively isn't just a skill; it's a form of social activism.

Overview of the Book's Structure and Key Themes

This book is designed to be more than just a read; it's a transformative journey. It's structured into three main parts, each exploring different facets of constructive conversation.

Part 1: Understanding the Terrain

The first part serves as your foundational guide. We'll investigate the nature of conflict and the emotional landscape that accompanies it. By understanding the dynamics at play, you'll be better equipped to navigate any argument or disagreement.

Part 2: The Toolbox

The second part is where you'll acquire your toolkit. This section is brimming with practical techniques—from the "Seek First to Understand" principle to the Socratic Method—that you can immediately apply in various conversational settings.

Part 3: Advanced Techniques and Application

The final part takes you into more complex territories, such as the art of apology and navigating difficult scenarios. We'll also explore how these principles apply in the digital age, where much of our communication now occurs.

Throughout the book, you'll encounter "Pit Stops for Reflection," designed to encourage introspection and active engagement with the material. These interactive elements make the journey a two-way dialogue, allowing for a deeper, more personalized experience.

At the end of this journey, you'll have more than just theoretical knowledge; you'll possess a robust set of practical skills and a changed perspective. The ultimate goal is to transform not just how you approach conflicts but how you engage with the world.

The Invitation

As you stand at the threshold of this journey, know that you're already taking the first step toward change—simply by recognizing the value of constructive conversation and seeking to improve your skills in it. Whether you consider yourself a seasoned communicator or someone who struggles to get their point across, this book offers something invaluable for everyone.

I invite you to embark on this journey with an open heart and mind. Leave behind your preconceptions and your fears. The pages that follow are more than just words; they're a catalyst for personal and societal transformation. Here, you'll find not just ideas, but tools; not just theories, but actionable steps.

This is not a path you'll walk alone. Together, we'll navigate the complexities of human interaction, turning conflicts into meaningful connections and disagreements into opportunities for growth. So take a deep breath, open the first chapter, and let's begin this incredible journey.

PART ONE
UNDERSTANDING THE TERRAIN

Chapter 1: The Nature of Conflict

"Peace is not the absence of conflict; it is the ability to handle conflict by peaceful means."

– Ronald Reagan

C onflict is one of life's great inevitabilities, as certain as the ebb and flow of the tides or the change of seasons. Yet, despite its universality, it remains one of the most misunderstood and feared aspects of human interaction. But what if we were to reframe how we view conflict? What if, instead of seeing it as an obstacle to be avoided, we viewed it as a landscape rich with opportunities for growth and connection?

In this chapter, we'll embark on an exploration of the multifaceted nature of conflict. We'll lay down foundational definitions, venture into the various arenas where conflict manifests, and debunk some of the most common misconceptions that cloud our understanding of this complex phenomenon. By the end of this chapter, you'll have a more nuanced understanding of what conflict is and isn't, equipping you with the insight needed to navigate disagreements in a more constructive manner.

Conflict: A Definition

At its most elemental level, conflict can be described as a collision of differing opinions, values, or interests. It's akin to two rivers meeting at a junction; each comes with its own speed, direction, and sediment, and their meeting creates turbulence. But this turbulence is not inherently bad; it's a natural outcome of difference, and how we navigate it determines whether the confluence becomes a source of destruction or a wellspring of new possibilities.

This simple definition serves as the bedrock for understanding conflict in its myriad forms. Just as no two rivers are identical, no two conflicts are the same. They vary in intensity, duration, and complexity, often shaped by an interplay of external circumstances and internal emotions.

Different Arenas: The Many Stages Where Conflict Plays Out

While the basic definition of conflict provides us with a foundational understanding, it's crucial to recognize that conflicts don't occur in a vacuum. They manifest in various arenas of our lives, each with its unique dynamics, stakes, and complexities. In this section, we'll journey through these different contexts, from the intimacy of personal relationships to the formality of workplace settings, and even the internal battles we wage within ourselves.

Personal Relationships

In our closest relationships—be it with a spouse, a family member, or a dear friend—conflict often carries an emotional weight that can't be ignored. Here, disagreements aren't just about opposing viewpoints; they touch upon our core values, expectations, and emotional needs.

Example

Take, for instance, a married couple, Sarah and Mark. They find themselves repeatedly arguing over how to manage their finances. While the surface issue appears to be about money, the real conflict is rooted in their differing values around security and freedom. Sarah values long-term savings and financial security, while Mark prioritizes experiences and living in the moment.

Potential Outcomes

Conflicts in personal relationships can lead to a range of outcomes. On the negative side, unresolved conflicts can fester, leading to emotional distance or even the end of the relationship. However, when navigated constructively, these conflicts can result in deeper emotional connection and mutual understanding.

Challenges and Opportunities

The primary challenge in personal relationships is the emotional weight that accompanies conflicts. Feelings of love, vulnerability, and personal history can make these disagreements highly charged. But therein also lies the opportunity: because of the emotional investment, there's a higher incentive to resolve conflicts in a way that strengthens the relationship. The very factors that make these conflicts challenging can also make the rewards of resolving them even more enriching.

Workplaces

The office or work environment is another common arena for conflict. Here, the stakes are different. It's not just about personal feelings but professional reputations, career advancement, and even financial stability. Conflicts at work often revolve around differing work styles, goals, or interpretations of organizational values.

Example

Imagine two co-workers, Emily and Robert, at odds over a project timeline. Emily, ever the planner, insists on adhering strictly to deadlines. Robert, on the other hand, values flexibility and believes that creativity shouldn't be rushed. The tension between them reaches a point where it starts affecting not just their collaboration but also the team's morale.

Potential Outcomes

Workplace conflicts can result in various outcomes. On the negative side, they can lead to a toxic work environment, decreased productivity, and even job loss. However, when managed well, these conflicts can lead to innovative solutions, improved work relationships, and a more cohesive team.

Challenges and Opportunities

The workplace presents unique challenges for conflict resolution. Hierarchies, office politics, and career implications can add layers of complexity to what might otherwise be a straightforward disagreement. However, the structured nature of the workplace also provides opportunities for constructive resolution, such as formal mediation processes or team-building activities. Navigating conflicts successfully here not only resolves the immediate issue but can also set a positive precedent for organizational culture.

Social Settings

From community gatherings to social media platforms, conflicts in broader social settings often involve a mix of personal and public stakes. These disagreements can range from casual debates over cultural or political issues to more significant disputes that can divide communities.

Example

Consider a neighborhood community meeting about implementing speed bumps on local roads. On one side, you have parents concerned about their children's safety. On the other, you have residents worried that speed bumps will lower property values. The disagreement escalates into a heated debate, causing rifts among neighbors.

Potential Outcomes

In social settings, conflicts can have a wide array of outcomes. At their worst, they can lead to community divisions, public shaming, or even violence. However, when handled constructively, they can result in community-driven solutions, stronger local bonds, and a more inclusive environment.

Challenges and Opportunities

Conflicts in social settings present unique challenges due to the diversity of stakeholders involved. The stakes are not just personal but communal, touching on shared values, resources, and public opinion. However, these settings also offer unique opportunities for community engagement and democratic decision-making. Successfully navigating conflict here can set the tone for more inclusive and cooperative community relationships moving forward.

Internal Conflict

Lastly, let's not overlook the battlefield within. Sometimes, the most challenging conflicts are those we have with ourselves. These internal struggles may involve ethical dilemmas, decisions about personal priorities, or emotional conflicts, such as guilt or regret.

Example

Imagine finding yourself at a career crossroads. One path leads to a high-paying job that aligns with your expertise but might demand long hours and significant stress. The other path leads to a role that pays less but offers a better work-life balance and aligns with your passions. The internal tug-of-war between financial security and personal fulfillment creates a conflict that can keep you awake at night.

Potential Outcomes

The outcomes of internal conflicts can vary dramatically. On one end, failing to resolve these conflicts can lead to chronic stress, indecision, and even emotional turmoil. On the other end, successfully navigating internal conflict can result in personal growth, a clarified sense of purpose, and a more satisfying life trajectory.

Challenges and Opportunities

The challenge with internal conflicts lies in the lack of external mediation. You are both the disputing parties and the mediator, making it easy to get stuck in a loop of indecision or rationalization. However, this also presents an opportunity for deep self-reflection and growth. Since you're the sole stakeholder, you have the freedom to explore various facets of the conflict without external pressures, allowing for a more nuanced resolution.

The Many Faces of Conflict: Understanding Its Types and Dynamics

Understanding conflict is not just about knowing where it happens but also recognizing the forms it can take. Conflicts are generally classified into three main types: interpersonal, intrapersonal, and group conflict. Let's explore each:

Interpersonal Conflict

Interpersonal conflict is what most people envision when they think of conflict—a clash between two or more individuals. These conflicts are often the most visible and emotionally charged, occurring in various contexts from personal relationships to professional environments and broader social settings.

The Dynamics

The dynamics of interpersonal conflict are influenced by a variety of factors, including personality traits, communication styles, and underlying values or beliefs. The emotional intensity can range from mild tension to full-blown emotional fireworks, depending on how invested each party is in the conflict and the topic at hand.

Examples and Scenarios

Take, for example, a disagreement between two close friends, Anna and Curtis, over political beliefs. What starts as a casual debate over coffee quickly escalates. Anna feels that Curtis is dismissing her viewpoints, while Curtis feels Anna is becoming too emotional. The conversation shifts from a discussion about politics to a battle of misunderstood intentions and hurt feelings.

Potential Outcomes

The outcomes of interpersonal conflicts are as varied as the conflicts themselves. When poorly managed, these disagreements can lead to fractured relationships and lingering resentment. However, when handled constructively, they offer an opportunity for deeper understanding, growth, and even strengthened relationships.

Challenges and Opportunities

One of the greatest challenges in interpersonal conflicts is emotional attachment. Because these conflicts often involve people we care about, emotions can run high, making rational discussion difficult. However, this emotional weight also offers an opportunity: it serves as a powerful motivator for resolution, pushing us to find common ground and mutual understanding.

Intrapersonal Conflict

Intrapersonal conflict is an internal tug-of-war, a clash within oneself. These conflicts often involve ethical dilemmas, decisions about personal priorities, or emotional struggles such as guilt or regret. Unlike interpersonal conflicts, these battles are often fought in solitude, making them less visible but no less significant.

The Dynamics

Intrapersonal conflicts often involve competing desires, values, or needs. For example, the desire for career advancement may conflict with the need for work-life balance. The lack of an external party means you serve as both the disputant and mediator, creating a unique dynamic that can be both empowering and paralyzing.

Examples and Scenarios

Consider the case of Jordan, who is offered a promotion with greater responsibilities but less personal time. On one hand, the promotion aligns with his career goals and provides financial benefits. On the other, it threatens his cherished work-life balance, potentially affecting his relationships and mental well-being.

Potential Outcomes

Left unresolved, intrapersonal conflicts can lead to chronic stress, indecision, and a diminished sense of well-being. However, when confronted and resolved, these conflicts offer a chance for personal growth, better self-understanding, and a clarified sense of purpose.

Challenges and Opportunities

The main challenge with intrapersonal conflict is its solitary nature, which can lead to prolonged indecision or emotional turmoil. However, this solitude also provides an opportunity for deep introspection. Without external influences, you're free to explore the depths of your conflict, gaining insights that can lead to more nuanced resolutions.

Group Conflict

Group conflict emerges when disagreements or tensions arise among members of a particular group, be it a family, a workplace team, or a community. Unlike interpersonal or intrapersonal conflicts, these involve more complex dynamics and can be influenced by a multitude of factors such as group norms, power structures, and even past histories among members.

The Dynamics

In group conflicts, the issue often goes beyond individual viewpoints to touch on collective values, goals, or resources. The presence of multiple stakeholders adds layers of complexity, as each individual may bring their unique perspective, biases, and interests to the table.

Examples and Scenarios

Imagine a project team at a tech company divided over the direction of a new product. One faction believes in sticking to the company's tried-and-true formula, while the other advocates for a more innovative, riskier approach. The conflict doesn't just affect the individuals involved but has implications for the entire project and, potentially, the company's future.

Potential Outcomes

Group conflicts can lead to a variety of outcomes. Poorly managed, they can result in reduced productivity, low morale, and a fragmented group dynamic. However, when addressed constructively, they offer an opportunity for collaborative problem-solving, enhanced group cohesion, and even organizational innovation.

Challenges and Opportunities

The challenges in resolving group conflicts often lie in the complexities of group dynamics, including issues of hierarchy, power imbalances, and differing communication styles. Yet, these conflicts also offer unique opportunities. A well-managed group conflict can serve as a catalyst for change, spurring the group to reevaluate outdated norms or practices and encouraging a more inclusive, collaborative environment.

Psychological Angles: A Glimpse Into the Mind's Role in Conflict

In our journey through the landscapes of conflict, it's essential to note that often the battleground isn't just external or interpersonal but also psychological. Concepts like cognitive dissonance, confirmation bias, and emotional triggers play significant roles in how conflicts are perceived, escalated, and ultimately resolved.

Cognitive Dissonance

For instance, cognitive dissonance occurs when we hold two conflicting beliefs simultaneously, leading to emotional discomfort. This psychological tension can fuel conflicts, especially when we're confronted with information or viewpoints that challenge our core beliefs.

Confirmation Bias

Another psychological factor is confirmation bias, our tendency to search for, interpret, and remember information that confirms our pre-existing beliefs. This bias can make us resistant to differing viewpoints, exacerbating conflicts.

Emotional Triggers

Lastly, emotional triggers are those specific words, actions, or situations that provoke an emotional response, often a strong one. Recognizing these triggers in ourselves and others can be crucial for managing conflicts effectively.

Common Misconceptions: Unveiling the Myths That Cloud Our Judgment

When it comes to conflict, misconceptions abound. These myths often serve as barriers to constructive resolution, leading us down paths of escalation rather than understanding. In this section, we'll demystify some of these common fallacies, setting the stage for a more enlightened approach to conflict.

Misconception 1: Conflict is Always Negative

One of the most pervasive myths is that conflict is inherently bad or negative. This belief can make us avoid conflict at all costs, often at the expense of addressing important issues.

The Reality

The truth is, conflict is not intrinsically negative. It's a natural part of human interaction and, when managed constructively, can serve as a catalyst for growth, innovation, and deeper relationships.

Why This Misconception Persists

This myth likely endures because of our emotional experiences with poorly managed conflicts, which can leave scars. Moreover, societal narratives often portray conflict as something to be avoided, reinforcing this misconception.

The Impact

The belief that conflict is always negative can lead to avoidance behaviors, stifling communication and growth. It can also create a self-fulfilling prophecy: if we enter a conflict believing it will end poorly, our actions and attitudes may make that outcome more likely.

Misconception 2: The Loudest Voice Wins

Another common misconception is that being loud, assertive, or even aggressive is the key to "winning" a conflict. This idea is often perpetuated by competitive cultures and environments that reward outspokenness over thoughtful dialogue.

The Reality

Contrary to this belief, volume does not equate to validity. A well-structured argument presented calmly often holds more weight than a loudly voiced but poorly reasoned one. Additionally, the goal in constructive conflict isn't to "win," but to arrive at a mutual understanding or solution.

Why This Misconception Persists

This myth is often reinforced by societal norms and media portrayals where the loudest or most dominant individual is viewed as the victor. It taps into a primal understanding of power dynamics, where the loudest roar in the animal kingdom often signifies dominance.

The Impact

Believing that loudness equals victory can lead to destructive communication styles. It can escalate conflicts unnecessarily and shut down opportunities for meaningful dialogue. This approach often leaves the quieter voices unheard, missing out on potentially valuable perspectives.

Misconception 3: The Avoidance Trap

The notion that avoiding conflict will make it go away or prevent emotional pain is another pervasive misconception. Many people choose to sidestep disagreements, thinking they're maintaining peace when, in reality, they're often allowing issues to fester.

The Reality

Avoiding conflict doesn't resolve it; it merely postpones it. While it may offer a temporary reprieve, avoidance often leads to a build-up of resentment or misunderstandings that can erupt more destructively later on.

Why This Misconception Persists

The allure of immediate peace is potent. It's the path of least resistance, appealing to our innate desire for harmony and our aversion to discomfort. This is why the avoidance trap is so easy to fall into; it offers the illusion of resolution without the emotional labor of confrontation.

The Impact

The cost of avoidance is high. Issues left unaddressed can grow, leading to larger, more complex conflicts down the line. Moreover, constant avoidance can create an environment of passive-aggressiveness and unspoken tension, eroding relationships and team dynamics over time.

Misconception 4: The Winner-Loser Paradigm

Many people approach conflict as if it's a zero-sum game, a battle where one person wins and the other loses. This competitive mindset is often ingrained from an early age, reinforced by societal norms, educational systems, and even sporting events.

The Reality

Conflict is rarely a zero-sum game. More often than not, it's an opportunity for collaboration and mutual growth. When we focus on winning or losing, we miss the chance to find solutions that could benefit both parties.

Why This Misconception Persists

The notion of life as a competition is deeply embedded in many cultures. From grades in school to promotions at work, we're often conditioned to see success as a finite resource to be claimed, fostering a winner-loser perspective.

The Impact

Approaching conflict with a winner-loser mindset narrows our vision, limiting the potential outcomes to those that serve our interests at the expense of others. It can lead to stubbornness, poor listening, and ultimately, missed opportunities for more meaningful resolutions and relationships.

Conflict as a Meeting Ground for Growth

As we've untangled the web of misconceptions surrounding conflict, we've begun to see glimmers of its untapped potential. Conflict is not just a battleground of opposing forces but can also be fertile ground for growth, learning, and relationship deepening. In this section, we'll explore how to reframe our understanding of conflict, turning it into an opportunity rather than an obstacle.

The Opportunity Lens: Reframing Our View of Conflict

Most people see conflict as a problem to solve, a hassle to get through, or even a threat to their well-being. This perspective, while understandable, limits our capacity to gain anything meaningful from these challenging situations.

Conflict, when approached with an open mind and constructive intent, can be a catalyst for growth. It provides a unique opportunity to learn not just about the other person's viewpoints, but also about our own biases, emotional triggers, and areas of ignorance. It's a mirror that reflects our character, showing us areas where we could improve.

Adopting the "opportunity lens" transforms how we engage in conflict. Instead of dreading it, we begin to see each disagreement as a chance to deepen our understanding, improve our relationships, and even grow as individuals.

When we view conflict as an opportunity, we're more likely to approach it with a constructive mindset, ready to listen, learn, and find common ground. This mindset shift doesn't just make the resolution process more enjoyable; it also often leads to more sustainable, mutually beneficial outcomes.

The Yin and Yang: Harmony in Duality

The ancient Chinese concept of yin and yang serves as a potent metaphor for understanding the dual nature of conflict. At its core, yin and yang represent two opposite yet complementary forces in the universe. Think of it like night and day, or water and fire. Each exists not in spite of but because of the other, and each brings out aspects of the other that wouldn't be visible otherwise.

In the context of conflict, the yin and yang metaphor helps us see how opposing ideas or interests can be complementary rather than adversarial. One viewpoint might focus on practical considerations (the yin), while the other emphasizes emotional or ethical aspects (the yang). Rather than canceling each other out, these perspectives can enhance the value of the other, leading to a richer, more nuanced understanding of the issue at hand.

The yin and yang metaphor encourages us to look for the value in opposing viewpoints, to seek the complementary force that makes our own perspective more complete. It nudges us toward a mindset of integration rather than division.

Applying the yin and yang perspective to conflicts can lead to more harmonious resolutions. It helps us step out of the zero-sum game mindset, opening us to solutions that honor both sides of the equation. In doing so, we not only resolve the issue at hand but often uncover new, unexpected opportunities for growth and connection.

The Crucible of Character: How Conflict Shapes Us

So far, we've explored the opportunities that conflict presents for growth and understanding, even using the yin and yang metaphor to illustrate the complementarity of opposing forces. Now, let's turn our attention inward, focusing on how conflict serves as a crucible for our own personal development.

Conflicts often bring us face to face with our deepest fears, insecurities, and vulnerabilities. But it's precisely in these uncomfortable moments that we have the opportunity to grow the most. Conflict acts as a spotlight, illuminating the corners of our personality that we might prefer to keep in the shadows.

Recognizing conflict as a crucible for character growth shifts our focus from external resolution to internal transformation. It encourages us to ask reflective questions like, "What is this conflict revealing about me?" or "What can I learn from this experience about my own reactions, judgments, or biases?"

When we view conflict as an opportunity for personal growth, we become more resilient, empathetic, and self-aware. These are qualities that not only aid in resolving the present conflict but also equip us to handle future challenges more effectively.

Real-Life Examples: From Friction to Flourishing

To truly appreciate the transformative power of conflict, it's valuable to examine instances where what seemed like a dire situation led to unexpectedly positive outcomes. Here, we'll share a few case studies that demonstrate the themes we've explored, from innovation and stronger relationships to personal growth.

Example 1: The Office Innovation

In a tech startup, two lead developers, Alex and Chris, clashed over how to approach a critical project. Alex was a proponent of rapid prototyping, while Chris advocated for a more methodical, research-based approach. The tension reached a boiling point in a team meeting, leading to a facilitated discussion between the two.

Rather than sticking to their corners, they decided to merge their approaches. The result was a groundbreaking hybrid methodology that not only resolved their conflict but also led to a significant innovation for the company.

Example 2: Strengthened Friendship

Two long-time friends, Maria and Naomi, found themselves at odds over political beliefs. Instead of letting the disagreement fester or avoiding it, they chose to engage in a series of open, respectful conversations. Through these talks, they not only found common ground but also deepened their understanding and respect for each other, strengthening their friendship in the process.

Example 3: Personal Growth Through Family Conflict

Tom found himself constantly butting heads with his teenage son, Jake, over curfew times and responsibilities around the house. Recognizing the pattern, Tom chose to approach the conflict as an opportunity for his own personal growth. He used the disagreements as a mirror, reflecting on his own tendencies to seek control. This introspection led to a more empathetic approach, ultimately improving his relationship with Jake and helping him grow as a parent.

Wrapping Up: The Many Facets of Conflict

As we conclude this chapter, it's worth reflecting on how our perception of conflict has evolved. We've journeyed from understanding the basic definitions and arenas where conflict occurs to debunking common misconceptions that often impede constructive dialogue. We've reframed conflict as not just an obstacle to navigate but an opportunity to seize, whether for personal growth, relationship building, or even innovation.

The real-life examples underscore the practical implications of adopting this enlightened perspective on conflict. They serve as a testament to the transformative power that lies within each disagreement, each clash of opinions, and each moment of tension.

By embracing conflict as a meeting ground for growth, we open ourselves to a myriad of opportunities that can enrich our lives in unexpected ways. And as we'll discover in the following chapters, the tools and strategies to harness this potential are within reach, waiting for us to grasp them and transform our approach to conflict forever.

Pit Stop for Reflection: Chapter 1

As we navigate this intricate landscape of conflict and constructive conversations, it's crucial to take moments to pause, reflect, and internalize what we've learned. Think of these "Pit Stops for Reflection" as mini rest stops along our journey—a place to catch your breath, take in the view, and prepare for the next leg. Here, you'll find reflective questions, thought exercises, and actionable steps designed to deepen your understanding and equip you for real-world application.

1. Reframing Your View: Think about a recent conflict you've experienced. How could viewing it through the "Opportunity Lens" change your perception of the situation?
2. The Yin and Yang in Your Life: Identify a conflict where you saw two opposing viewpoints as entirely adversarial. Could these perspectives be complementary, like yin and yang? How?
3. Character Growth: Reflect on a past disagreement and consider what it revealed about your character. What did you learn about your emotional triggers, biases, or areas needing growth?
4. Real-World Application: Is there a current conflict in your life where you could apply what you've learned in this chapter? Outline a brief action plan for how you might approach it differently.

Chapter 2: The Emotional Landscape

"The single biggest problem in communication is the illusion that it has taken place."

– George Bernard Shaw

If Chapter 1 was about understanding the 'what' and 'where' of conflict, welcome now to the 'why'—the emotional undercurrents that drive the ebb and flow of every argument, disagreement, and confrontation. You see, while the mechanics of conflict might be navigated with reason and logic, the fuel that often feeds these conflicts is undeniably emotional.

In this chapter, we're going to explore the complex tapestry of human emotions that lies at the heart of most conflicts. We'll look into the psychology of emotions, introduce the pivotal role of Emotional Intelligence (EI), and discuss how understanding emotional triggers can transform the way we approach conflicts.

In navigating the labyrinth of human interactions, understanding the emotional dynamics at play can be your guiding light. It can help you defuse tension, foster understanding, and even turn potential breakdowns into breakthroughs.

The Psychology of Emotions in Conflicts

Imagine walking into a room where an argument is underway. Even if you don't immediately catch the words being exchanged, you can feel the tension in the air. It's like an electric charge, a palpable force that seems to buzz around the room. That charge? It's an amalgam of basic human emotions—anger, fear, sadness—each contributing its unique voltage to the overall current of the conflict.

Anger often takes center stage, a blazing fire fueled by perceived injustices or unmet expectations. It's the voice that shouts, demands to be heard, and, at its worst, seeks to overpower.

Fear lurks in the background, a shadowy figure that whispers uncertainties and magnifies risks. It can make us defensive, evasive, or even aggressive, all in a bid to protect ourselves from perceived threats, whether real or imagined.

Sadness, on the other hand, is the quiet observer. It's the emotion that often arrives after the heat of the moment, when the smoke clears and you're left assessing the emotional wreckage. It's the feeling of loss, of missed opportunities for connection, understanding, or resolution.

These emotions, while basic, wield immense power in shaping the nature and outcome of conflicts. By recognizing them, understanding their origins, and learning how they manifest in our behavior, we're taking the first crucial step in managing conflicts more effectively.

The Amygdala Hijack: When Emotion Overwhelms Reason

You've likely experienced a moment where your emotional response was so intense it felt as if you were being overtaken. Maybe you snapped at a colleague during a meeting, or perhaps you slammed the door during a heated argument with a loved one. It's as if your rational self stepped aside, allowing this emotional whirlwind to seize control. What you've experienced is commonly known as an "amygdala hijack."

At the core of this emotional coup d'état is a small almond-shaped cluster of nuclei in your brain known as the amygdala. While the amygdala has multiple functions, one of its primary roles is to act as a sort of emotional processing center, especially for fear-based responses. When you perceive a threat—be it a snide comment or a confrontational tone—your amygdala can trigger a flood of stress hormones, effectively hijacking your rational brain.

The immediate impact of an amygdala hijack in a conflict scenario is often damaging. Communication breaks down, defensive walls go up, and the opportunity for constructive dialogue dwindles. It's like throwing a match into a room filled with gasoline fumes; the resulting explosion can be both immediate and devastating.

Recognizing the signs of an impending amygdala hijack is the first step in mitigating its impact. The rapid heartbeat, the flushed face, the tunnel vision—all are cues that your emotional brain is about to seize the reins. By identifying these symptoms early, you can employ techniques, such as deep breathing or stepping away momentarily, to let your rational brain catch up and regain control.

By understanding the mechanics and implications of the amygdala hijack, you arm yourself with invaluable knowledge. This insight allows you to be more aware, not just of your own emotional triggers, but also of the emotional dynamics unfolding during conflicts.

Fight, Flight, or Freeze: The Primal Reactions in Modern-Day Conflicts

When confronted with a threat—real or perceived—our bodies have been wired through millennia of evolution to react in one of three ways: fight, flight, or freeze. These are not mere choices we consciously make; they are deeply ingrained survival mechanisms, orchestrated by our brain and executed before we even have time to think.

The "fight" response is perhaps the most visceral and immediate. It's the urge to push back, to assert oneself, and to confront the threat head-on. In modern-day conflicts, this may not mean physical aggression but could manifest as raised voices, sharp rebuttals, or even the compulsion to have the last word. This is where your inner warrior takes the stage, sword unsheathed, ready for battle.

Then there's "flight," which is the instinct to remove oneself from the danger zone as quickly as possible. In today's world, this can translate into avoiding eye contact, leaving the room, or even cutting off relationships. It's the art of tactical withdrawal, a retreat to regroup or, at times, to avoid confrontation altogether.

The "freeze" response is perhaps the least understood but equally significant. It's that moment of paralysis, the sensation of being a deer caught in headlights. In conflicts, this might mean going silent, failing to articulate your thoughts, or feeling emotionally stuck. While it may seem counterproductive, freezing can be a protective mechanism, buying time as your mind subconsciously assesses the situation.

Most people have a default setting, a go-to reaction they're more inclined to exhibit during conflicts. Identifying yours can be a revelation, offering you not just self-awareness but a roadmap to how you can better

28

manage conflicts. For example, if you know you're prone to the "fight" response, learning de-escalation techniques can be particularly beneficial.

Understanding these primal reactions allows us to see conflicts through a new lens, one that recognizes the instinctive, almost automatic ways we react. This self-awareness opens the door to greater emotional intelligence and offers us more constructive ways to engage in disagreements.

The Psychological and Physiological Toll of Unmanaged Emotions

While the immediate consequences of poorly managed emotions in conflict are evident—strained relationships, loss of trust, missed opportunities—the long-term implications can be far-reaching and, in some cases, devastating. They manifest not only in our mental well-being but also in the very fabric of our physical health.

Psychologically, the fallout of unmanaged emotions can be like a dark cloud that looms over your life. Symptoms of anxiety, depression, and chronic stress often find their roots in unresolved conflicts and uncontrolled emotional reactions. Over time, these mental health challenges can affect your self-esteem, your ability to form and maintain relationships, and even your professional life.

But the costs don't stop there. Our bodies are intricately connected to our emotional states. The stress hormones released during conflicts—cortisol and adrenaline, among others—have a direct impact on various bodily systems. Elevated cortisol levels over prolonged periods can lead to issues like digestive problems, insomnia, and an increased risk of chronic diseases like heart disease and diabetes.

In a sense, poorly managed emotions can act like a poison, seeping into various aspects of your life, often in ways you might not immediately recognize. Therefore, understanding how to manage emotional responses in conflict isn't just a skill for effective communication; it's a vital component of holistic well-being.

The good news is that these costs are not inevitable. As we journey through this book, we'll explore strategies, tools, and mindsets that can help you manage your emotional landscape more effectively, thereby reducing the psychological and physiological toll it can take.

Introducing Emotional Intelligence and Its Relevance

Think of Emotional Intelligence as your emotional GPS. Just as a GPS helps you navigate unfamiliar roads, EI equips you with the skills to navigate the complex emotional landscapes within and around you. Simply put, Emotional Intelligence is the ability to understand and manage your own emotions, as well as the ability to tune into and influence the emotions of others.

Understanding your emotions means being aware of what you're feeling and why you're feeling it. It's the self-awareness that allows you to recognize when you're on the verge of an amygdala hijack or when your 'fight, flight, or freeze' instincts are kicking in.

Managing your emotions, on the other hand, involves making conscious choices about how you react. It's the skill that lets you take a deep breath and choose a thoughtful response over a knee-jerk reaction.

But EI doesn't stop at the borders of your own emotional world; it extends into understanding the emotions of others. This is where empathy comes into play, allowing you to perceive someone else's emotional state, even when it's not explicitly stated. And once you understand what someone else is feeling, you have the key to influencing not just their emotional state but also the overall emotional climate of a situation.

Emotional Intelligence isn't just a nice-to-have skill; it's an essential one, especially when it comes to conflicts. It's the tool that turns you from a passive participant in an emotional rollercoaster to an active, skilled driver on an emotional highway.

The Four Pillars of Emotional Intelligence

Self-Awareness: The Mirror to Your Emotional Self

The first pillar, self-awareness, is the cornerstone upon which the other pillars stand. It's the ability to look inward and recognize your own emotional states. This internal mirror allows you to understand why you feel the way you do and how those feelings can affect your actions. Being self-aware in conflict means catching the early signs of emotional escalation, thereby giving you the chance to navigate the situation more skillfully.

Self-Management: The Emotional Steering Wheel

Once you're aware of your emotions, the next step is managing them, which brings us to the second pillar: self-management. Think of this as your emotional steering wheel. You can't control the traffic around you, but you can control how you navigate through it. This is the skill that enables you to stay calm under pressure, think more clearly, and choose responses that align with your values and objectives.

Social Awareness: The Compass of Interpersonal Relationships

The third pillar, social awareness, is the extension of self-awareness into the social realm. It's your emotional compass, guiding you through the emotional landscapes of others. In conflicts, social awareness enables you to read the room, to sense the emotional currents running through a conversation, and to adapt your approach accordingly.

Relationship Management: The Bridge to Harmonious Interactions

The final pillar, relationship management, is where all the previous skills come together in a symphony of interpersonal effectiveness. This is the art of managing interactions, resolving conflicts, and inspiring others. In a conflict situation, relationship management involves finding common ground, fostering understanding, and building a bridge between opposing viewpoints.

Understanding these four pillars is akin to having a toolkit for emotional intelligence. Each tool serves its unique purpose, and when used in harmony, they enable you to navigate conflicts with a level of skill and nuance that transforms them into opportunities for growth and connection.

Emotional Intelligence in Conflict: The Game-Changer

When you find yourself embroiled in a disagreement, whether it's a heated debate with a friend or a tense negotiation at work, Emotional Intelligence isn't just an asset; it's a game-changer. Let's examine how each of the four pillars comes into play during conflicts.

Self-awareness acts like an internal warning system. Imagine you're in the middle of an argument, and you feel your heart rate start to climb, your palms get sweaty, or perhaps you notice a tightness in your chest. These are your body's cues that you're entering the emotional red zone. Being self-aware allows you to recognize these signs early on, offering you a critical moment to pause and choose a more constructive response.

This is where self-management kicks in. Once you're aware you're getting heated, you can employ various techniques to cool down. Maybe it's taking a deep breath, counting to ten, or temporarily stepping away from the situation. This ability to manage your emotional state serves as a buffer against escalation, keeping the conflict from spiraling out of control.

In conflicts, being socially aware means you're not just tuned into your emotional radio station but also into the other person's. You're attentive to their body language, their tone, and their words, which gives you valuable insights into their emotional state. This heightened awareness can guide your responses in a way that fosters mutual understanding rather than further discord.

Finally, when it comes to managing the relationship, Emotional Intelligence allows you to navigate the situation like a skilled diplomat. You defuse tension by finding common ground, validating the other person's feelings, and seeking a resolution that respects both parties' needs and concerns. It's the dance of de-escalation, where you lead with empathy and follow with resolution.

By harnessing the power of Emotional Intelligence, you turn conflicts into fertile ground for deeper understanding, stronger relationships, and personal growth. This shift in perspective doesn't just change how you engage in conflicts; it changes the outcome, transforming them from battles to be won into opportunities for mutual growth.

Emotional Triggers and How to Identify Them

Emotional triggers are like invisible tripwires in our minds. They are specific events, words, or situations that evoke a strong emotional response, often without us fully understanding why. You can think of them as buttons that, when pushed, play a pre-recorded emotional message inside us. Whether it's a sarcastic remark from a colleague, a specific tone of voice, or even a particular topic of discussion, triggers have the power to rapidly escalate our emotional state.

Now, you might wonder, why do these triggers exist? Well, they often originate from past experiences, conditioning, or emotional traumas. They're like echoes from our past, resounding loudly in the present, often out of context. In conflicts, triggers act as accelerators; they speed up the emotional timeline, making zero-to-sixty escalation happen in mere seconds.

Recognizing your triggers is like mapping out these invisible tripwires. Once you know where they are, you can navigate more carefully, avoiding unnecessary emotional explosions.

Common Emotional Triggers in Conflicts

While triggers are deeply personal and can vary widely from person to person, there are some emotional tripwires that are common across many individuals. Recognizing these can serve as a starting point for your own exploration into what sets off your emotional alarms. Here are some examples:

Feeling Disrespected

One of the most powerful triggers for many people is the feeling of being disrespected. Whether it's an offhand comment that belittles your contributions or an overt act of undermining, the feeling of disrespect can ignite a firestorm of emotion.

Being Ignored

Another common trigger is the sense that you're being ignored or dismissed. In conflicts, this can manifest as someone talking over you, disregarding your input, or outright ignoring your presence. The emotional toll can be both profound and immediate, escalating the conflict unnecessarily.

Feeling Threatened

The sensation of being threatened, either physically or emotionally, can also be a significant trigger. This often leads to a 'fight or flight' response, narrowing your focus and reducing your ability to think clearly or engage constructively in the disagreement.

Feeling Controlled

For many, the notion of someone else controlling them or their circumstances can act as a trigger. Whether it's being told what to do, having choices made for you, or feeling micromanaged, this can evoke strong feelings of rebellion or resentment.

Perceived Injustice

The feeling that you're being treated unfairly or that there's an imbalance of power can also be a potent trigger. This could be a skewed division of household chores, being passed over for a promotion, or feeling like your voice isn't being heard in a group setting.

Rejection or Exclusion

Being left out, excluded, or outright rejected can be deeply triggering for many people. In a conflict, if someone dismisses your opinion or excludes you from a decision-making process, it can evoke feelings of inadequacy or even abandonment.

These common triggers act as emotional landmines, often setting off an explosion of feelings that can derail a conversation. The key to navigating them is recognition—both of your own triggers and potentially those of others involved in the conflict.

By identifying these common triggers, you're taking the first step toward disarming them. The next phase is learning how to navigate around them or defuse them, which we'll explore as we move deeper into this chapter.

The Power of Naming: Your Emotional Circuit Breaker

Have you ever noticed that the moment you can name what you're feeling, it somehow feels less overwhelming? This isn't just a psychological trick; it's rooted in neuroscience. When you name an emotion—whether it's anger, frustration, or anxiety—you're activating the prefrontal cortex, the rational part of your brain, and reducing activity in the amygdala, the emotional center. It's like flipping a switch that moves you from reactive to reflective.

Techniques for Identifying Your Triggers

So how do you put this into practice, especially in the heat of a conflict? Here are some techniques:

1. Pause and Breathe: The first step is to pause and take a deep breath. This physical act alone can help disrupt the emotional hijack.
2. Ask Yourself: In that paused moment, ask yourself, "What am I feeling right now?" Try to be as specific as possible. Are you angry,

or is it more like indignation? Are you anxious, or is it more a sense of dread?

3. Label Out Loud: If appropriate and it won't escalate the situation, consider naming the emotion out loud. Say, "I'm feeling really frustrated right now." This can also serve to alert the other party to your emotional state, opening the door for a more empathetic interaction.

4. Reflect on the Trigger: Once you've named the emotion, try to identify what triggered it. Was it something the other person said? A tone of voice? An implication?

By using these techniques, you're not just identifying your emotional triggers; you're also gaining the upper hand over them. It's akin to turning on the lights in a dark room. Suddenly, the obstacles that could trip you up become visible, and you can navigate around them more effectively.

The Trigger Journal: Your Personal Emotional Map

One of the most effective ways to become intimately acquainted with your emotional triggers is through journaling. Think of this as your personal emotional cartography project, mapping out the landscapes that can either lead you astray or toward a more enlightened path.

The Exercise

Here's how it works:

1. Identify the Trigger: Each time you find yourself in a situation where you feel a strong emotional reaction, jot it down. Describe what happened, who was involved, and where it took place.

2. Label the Emotion: Next, name the emotion you felt. Was it anger, frustration, fear, or perhaps a combination?

3. Analyze the Why: Try to dig deeper into why this particular situation triggered this emotion. Was it a specific comment, a tone, or perhaps a broader context like timing or location?

4. Note the Intensity: On a scale of 1 to 10, how intense was your emotional reaction? This can help you identify which triggers might require more immediate attention.

5. Reflect on the Response: Finally, write down how you reacted. Did you engage constructively, or did the emotion take the reins?

The Benefits

The benefits of keeping a Trigger Journal are multifaceted:

- Self-Awareness: You become more self-aware, understanding your emotional patterns and their roots.
- Control: Over time, you'll notice that simply writing about these triggers will give you a greater sense of control over them.
- Communication: It provides a language and framework to discuss emotional reactions in your relationships, making it easier to address issues before they escalate.

By consistently documenting your experiences in a Trigger Journal, you're not just gaining insights into your emotional makeup; you're also equipping yourself with the tools to navigate future conflicts more effectively. Think of this journal as your personal emotional GPS, guiding you through the intricate highways and byways of your emotional world.

Wrapping Up: Mastering Your Emotional Landscape

Throughout this chapter, we've ventured deep into the emotional terrain that forms the backdrop of every conflict. We've explored the primal emotions that often fuel disagreements, the psychological phenomena like the amygdala hijack, and the essential role of Emotional Intelligence. We also took a closer look at emotional triggers, those invisible tripwires that can escalate conflicts, often without our conscious understanding.

But remember, the journey doesn't stop here. The insights gained in this chapter are not just theoretical; they are profoundly practical. From learning to name your emotions to keeping a Trigger Journal, you now have a toolkit to help you become a more emotionally intelligent participant in any conflict.

Our emotional landscape isn't a battlefield to conquer but a rich, complex world to understand and navigate. And the better you understand this world, the more skilled you'll become at transforming conflicts into opportunities for growth, connection, and understanding.

Pit Stop for Reflection: Emotional Check-In

Before you turn the page to embark on the next part of this journey, let's take a moment to pause and reflect. This is your "pit stop" for emotional self-examination, where you can check your emotional "tire pressure," so to speak, and refuel your awareness tank.

Use this pit stop as a moment for genuine reflection. Your answers don't need to be perfect; they just need to be honest. The more you engage with these exercises and questions, the more you'll get out of the journey ahead.

Questions for Self-Reflection

1. Which Emotion Dominates?: Think about a recent conflict you were involved in. What was the dominant emotion you felt? Was it one of the basic emotions we discussed, or something more complex?
2. Trigger Identification: Can you identify a specific trigger from that conflict? Would you have recognized it without this chapter's insights?
3. Your Reaction Style: In general, do you tend to fight, flee, or freeze during conflicts? How has this affected the outcomes?
4. Emotional Intelligence Quotient: On a scale of 1 to 10, how would you rate your current level of Emotional Intelligence? Where do you see room for improvement?
5. Journaling Feasibility: Is the idea of keeping a Trigger Journal appealing to you? Why or why not?

Exercises

Name That Emotion: The next time you find yourself in a tense situation, practice the "Name That Emotion" technique. How does it change the dynamic?

Trigger Journal Entry: If you've decided to keep a Trigger Journal, make your first entry. Reflect on the process and how it makes you feel.

Chapter 3: The Mirror of Empathy

"Emotional intelligence begins with what is most personal to you—what you're saying to yourself."

– Travis Bradberry

Imagine standing in front of a mirror that reflects not just your physical features, but your emotional essence as well. What would you see? Would the reflection be clouded by biases, fears, and judgments, or would it emanate understanding, openness, and compassion? Welcome to the third milestone of our journey—exploring the mirror of empathy.

We've navigated the treacherous terrains of emotional landscapes and equipped ourselves with the toolkit of Emotional Intelligence. Now, it's time to venture into the realm of empathy, the magical mirror that reflects not just our own emotions but the inner world of those around us.

Empathy is like a bridge—sturdy yet flexible, allowing for the ebb and flow of human emotions, connecting two souls separated by the chasms of personal experiences and perspectives. It's more than a skill; it's an art form that, when mastered, can turn even the most volatile conflicts into opportunities for deep connection and mutual growth.

In this chapter, we'll demystify the neuroscience behind empathy, confront the barriers that obstruct our empathetic capabilities, and provide you with practical tools to become a more empathetic listener and communicator.

But before we dive into the science and the strategies, let's take a moment to reflect. Ask yourself:

- How do I usually respond when someone shares their feelings or concerns with me?

- Can I recall a time when empathy—or the lack of it—made a significant impact on the outcome of a conflict?

Prepare yourself for an enlightening journey through the mirror of empathy, where you'll not only see your reflection but also the reflections of those around you.

Exploring the Concept of Empathy

When someone says, "I feel you," what does that really mean? It's more than just a casual phrase; it's an expression of empathy. Empathy is the ability to understand and share the feelings of another person, almost like mental and emotional teleportation. You momentarily step out of your own experience and into theirs. It's the difference between looking at a painting and feeling the emotions that inspired each brushstroke.

Imagine, for a moment, that you're watching a close friend cry after a difficult breakup. Sympathy would say, "I'm sorry you're feeling this way," but empathy would say, "I'm here with you, feeling this pain alongside you." Sympathy observes; empathy participates.

The nuance lies in the depth of emotional engagement. Sympathy is like standing on the shore, empathizing with someone struggling in the water. Empathy, on the other hand, is diving in to join them, even if you can't necessarily save them.

But why is empathy so important, particularly in conflicts? Well, when you can see the world through another's eyes, it opens up pathways for deeper understanding, paving the way for constructive conversation and, eventually, resolution.

Now that we've defined empathy let's explore its various types.

Types of Empathy

Empathy isn't a one-size-fits-all concept; it comes in different flavors, each with its own unique impact on how we navigate conflicts. Let's explore the three primary types: cognitive, emotional, and compassionate empathy.

Cognitive Empathy

This is the Sherlock Holmes version of empathy, where you understand what the other person is thinking but may not necessarily feel

39

what they're feeling. Cognitive empathy is like being a skilled translator of someone's thoughts, decoding their words and behaviors into understandable terms. In a conflict, this enables you to grasp the other person's point of view intellectually, even if you don't emotionally resonate with it.

Emotional Empathy

Here, you don't just understand; you feel. Emotional empathy is like sinking your feet into someone else's emotional mud. You experience their joy, their pain, their hopes, and their fears as if they were your own. In conflicts, this can be both a gift and a challenge. While it fosters a deep emotional connection, it can also be draining and may cloud your judgment.

Compassionate Empathy

This is empathy in action. It's not just understanding someone's feelings or sharing them; it's also about being moved to help, if needed. Imagine a friend is grieving; compassionate empathy would involve not just understanding or sharing their grief but also helping them make funeral arrangements or just being there to listen. In conflicts, compassionate empathy can drive you to find a solution that benefits all parties involved.

Each type of empathy has its role in conflicts. Cognitive empathy helps you understand the other person's viewpoint, emotional empathy allows you to connect on a deeper level, and compassionate empathy propels you towards a constructive resolution.

In our next section, we'll differentiate empathy from its close but fundamentally different cousin, sympathy.

Empathy vs. Sympathy

When someone is going through a tough time, it's common to hear phrases like, "I feel for you," or, "I'm so sorry this happened." While these expressions seem empathetic, they often fall into the category of sympathy. Although both empathy and sympathy are responses to another person's suffering, they serve different roles in emotional connection and conflict resolution.

Think of sympathy as being the passive observer in a theater production. You're in the audience, watching the drama unfold, perhaps even shedding a tear at the poignant moments. But once the curtain falls, you go home, emotionally unscathed.

Empathy, on the other hand, is like being an actor on the stage, living each line, feeling each emotion, and understanding the role of every character. It's a more immersive and engaged experience. In the context of conflict, this means you're not just acknowledging the other person's feelings; you're sharing in them, which often leads to a deeper, more meaningful resolution.

Sympathy tends to keep emotional distance; it's a pat on the back, a comforting word, or a bouquet of "Get Well Soon" flowers. While these gestures are kind, they don't necessarily foster a deep emotional connection.

Empathy digs deeper. It's the hug that says, "I'm here for you," or the attentive listening that communicates, "I want to understand your perspective." In conflicts, this deeper connection often breaks down walls and fosters an environment where real resolution can occur.

With this distinction in mind, let's gear up to explore the fascinating science behind empathy and how our brain plays a pivotal role in this emotional capability.

The Neuroscientific Basis of Empathy

Science doesn't just explain the "how" of things; it often illuminates the "why," deepening our appreciation for phenomena we might otherwise take for granted. Empathy is no exception. When we venture into the labyrinth of the human brain, we find a complex network of cells and chemicals working in harmony to make empathy possible. Let's start by talking about a unique set of brain cells that scientists believe are central to our ability to empathize: mirror neurons.

Mirror Neurons

Have you ever winced when someone else stubbed their toe or felt your heart swell when you witnessed a touching reunion? These reactions can largely be attributed to mirror neurons. These specialized cells in the brain essentially allow us to "mirror" the emotional and physical experiences of others, offering a biological basis for empathy.

Imagine you're watching a tense scene in a movie where the main character is anxious. Your palms start to sweat, and you feel that same tension, almost as if you're right there with them. This is your brain's mirror neuron system at work, offering you a sample of the character's emotional state.

Mirror neurons aren't just about making you feel what someone else feels; they also help you understand the intent behind their actions. If someone raises their hand in a meeting, you're not just noticing the motion—you're comprehending that they have something to say. It's like having a built-in empathy radar in your brain.

Brain Chemistry

While mirror neurons might be the actors on the stage of empathy, brain chemistry is the behind-the-scenes crew, managing the lighting, sound, and special effects that make the performance come alive. One chemical that plays a starring role is oxytocin, often referred to as the "love hormone" or "cuddle chemical."

Oxytocin is released during moments of social bonding—like hugging a loved one or sharing a meaningful conversation. This hormone enhances our ability to empathize by fine-tuning our social radar, making us more attuned to the emotions of others. When oxytocin levels rise, barriers seem to melt away, paving the way for more authentic emotional connections.

Imagine you're at a family gathering that started off tense because of past misunderstandings. As the evening wears on, people start to relax, share stories, laugh, and maybe even hug. These actions stimulate the release of oxytocin, which in turn amplifies feelings of trust and emotional closeness, facilitating a more empathetic environment.

While oxytocin receives a lot of attention, it's not working alone. Other neurotransmitters like dopamine, which is associated with pleasure and reward, and serotonin, linked to well-being and happiness, also contribute to the empathetic responses in our brain.

Think of these chemicals as the different instruments in an orchestra, each playing its own part but contributing to a harmonious whole. In the context of conflict, this internal symphony can turn what started as a discordant exchange into a more harmonious dialogue.

The Empathy Circuit

When we talk about empathy, we're not just referring to a single "empathy center" in the brain. Instead, it's more like an intricate circuit—multiple regions each playing their role and communicating with each other to produce what we experience as empathic understanding.

Two key players in this empathy circuit are the pre-frontal cortex, the brain's executive center, and the limbic system, the emotional hub. The pre-frontal cortex helps us regulate emotional responses, ensuring we don't become overwhelmed during emotionally charged situations. The limbic system, on the other hand, is what allows us to feel emotions in the first place. It's a delicate balance between the two: too much emotional regulation, and you come off as cold; too little, and you're lost in your own emotions, unable to connect with others.

Imagine two dancers gracefully moving across a stage, each in tune with the other's movements. The pre-frontal cortex and limbic system are like these dancers, maintaining a delicate balance to ensure our empathic responses are both genuine and manageable. When faced with conflict, this dance becomes crucial. A misstep—like an overactive limbic system—can lead to emotional outbursts, while a lethargic pre-frontal cortex may result in emotional detachment.

In essence, empathy isn't the work of a lone actor or even a duo; it's a collaborative effort, a sophisticated dance involving multiple brain regions, each contributing its unique abilities to help us connect with others.

Barriers to Empathy and How to Overcome Them

Empathy may seem like a natural, even involuntary, response, but sometimes our own emotions can act as barriers. Judgment, fear, or past trauma can cloud our ability to empathize with others, especially in situations of conflict.

Imagine you're discussing a sensitive topic with a friend and they say something that triggers a painful memory. Suddenly, you're not just dealing with the present conflict; you're also grappling with emotions from your past. In moments like these, emotional blocks can hijack our empathic abilities, making us reactive rather than responsive.

We're not just products of our biology; we're also shaped by our environment. Cultural norms and social conditioning can have a profound influence on our ability to empathize. In some societies, showing emotion may be considered a sign of weakness, which can stifle empathic responses. Alternatively, some cultures place a high value on community and collective well-being, which can enhance empathic abilities.

Have you ever caught yourself making assumptions about someone based on their background or appearance? These cultural and societal lenses can distort our empathic vision, making it harder to connect on a genuine emotional level.

Overcoming Barriers

Empathy is like a muscle—it strengthens with practice. And just like physical workouts can break down barriers to physical fitness, certain practices can help us overcome emotional and social roadblocks to empathy.

Mindfulness Practices

Being present is the first step in being empathetic. Mindfulness techniques, such as deep breathing or grounding exercises, can help calm your mind and make you more receptive to others' feelings. The next time you find yourself in a heated discussion, try taking a few deep breaths to center yourself before responding. This simple act can shift your focus from reactive to empathetic.

Active Listening

Most of us listen to respond, not to understand. Active listening is about fully focusing, understanding, and remembering what the other person is saying. It involves not just hearing the words, but also understanding the emotions behind them. This can be especially useful in conflicts where emotions run high and every word counts.

Reframing Techniques

Sometimes, all it takes to break down a barrier is a change in perspective. If you catch yourself making assumptions or jumping to conclusions during a conflict, try to reframe the situation. Instead of seeing the other person as an opponent, view them as a collaborator in finding a solution.

The Empathy Workout

Just like a physical workout targets specific muscles, the Empathy Workout aims to flex and strengthen various aspects of your empathic abilities. These exercises aren't meant to be one-offs; they're practices you can incorporate into your daily life for ongoing growth.

Role-Playing Scenarios

Create a safe space with a trusted friend or family member to role-play different conflict scenarios. One of you can play the role of the "empathy challenger," throwing out statements that are tough to empathize with. The other person, the "empathy trainee," tries to respond with as much empathy as possible. After each round, discuss what worked and what didn't.

Empathy Journaling

Keep an "Empathy Journal" to track your emotional responses to conflicts or challenging interactions. Note down the situation, your initial emotional reaction, and how you chose to respond. Reflect on what barriers to empathy came up for you and how you might navigate them differently in the future.

The Empathy Timeout

In moments of high tension or conflict, give yourself permission to take an "Empathy Timeout." Step back from the situation—physically, if possible, or mentally if not—and take a few minutes to practice mindfulness or active listening techniques. Then return to the conversation with a refreshed, empathetic perspective.

These exercises aren't just theoretical; they're practical tools you can start using right away to deepen your empathic abilities.

Excellent! Incorporating these exercises into your routine is the key to making empathy not just an occasional practice, but a consistent way of interacting with the world. So, let's discuss how to seamlessly integrate these "workouts" into your daily life.

Integrating the Empathy Workout into Your Routine

The beauty of these exercises is that they can be tailored to fit any lifestyle. Here are some tips to make them a regular part of your routine:

The key to any successful routine is consistency. Choose a time each day to practice one of these empathy-building exercises. It could be during your morning coffee, right before bed, or even during your commute. The point is to make it a habit.

Set aside time each week to review your Empathy Journal. Reflect on your progress, identify areas for improvement, and celebrate your successes, no matter how small. These weekly check-ins serve as both a progress report and a source of motivation.

Share your empathy-building journey with someone you trust. An accountability partner can offer you feedback, encouragement, and even participate in the role-playing scenarios. Plus, it's easier to stick to a new routine when you know someone else is cheering you on.

Break down your empathy goals into smaller, achievable tasks. Instead of aiming to be more empathetic in all your relationships right away, start with one relationship or one type of interaction and build from there.

Lastly, don't overlook the conflicts and challenging interactions that naturally occur in your life. These are your real-world training grounds. After each conflict, take a few minutes to reflect on how you employed empathy and what you could do better next time.

By integrating these exercises into your routine, you're not just learning about empathy; you're living it. This isn't just an exercise for your mind, but a workout for your soul.

Wrapping Up: Understanding Empathy

By this point, you've not only gained a robust understanding of what empathy is but you've also looked into its neurological underpinnings and the barriers that can obstruct it. More importantly, you now have a set of practical exercises and a plan to make empathy an integral part of your daily life.

Understanding empathy is like knowing the mechanics of a car. It's helpful, sure, but it's only when you slide into the driver's seat and turn the key that you truly understand what it can do. The road ahead is filled with opportunities for meaningful connections, deeper understanding, and personal growth. All it takes is the courage to step on the gas.

Pit Stop for Reflection

As we wrap up this chapter, take a moment to reflect on your own experiences with empathy:

1. Can you recall a time when empathy—or a lack thereof—played a pivotal role in a personal conflict?
2. Are there particular barriers you've identified in yourself that might make practicing empathy more challenging?
3. Which exercise are you most excited to try out, and why?

Your answers to these questions are your road signs, guiding you as you navigate the winding roads of human interaction and conflict. Keep them close; they'll serve you well on the journey ahead.

Interlude: A Reflective Exercise

Welcome to the Interlude—a well-deserved pause in your journey through the intricacies of conflict and communication. Think of this as your personal basecamp where you can catch your breath, reflect on the miles you've covered, and prepare for the climbs ahead. Why now, you might ask? You've just completed Part I, which laid the groundwork for understanding the emotional and empathic facets of conflict. It's easy to breeze through these chapters, nodding in agreement or pondering the examples. However, it's quite another thing to apply these insights to your own life. That's what this Interlude aims to help you do.

So, what's on the agenda for this Interlude? We have two primary exercises designed to help you engage more deeply with the topics of emotional triggers and empathy. Each exercise is structured to provide you with reflective questions and practical steps. You can expect to spend anywhere from 20 minutes to an hour on these exercises, depending on how deep you wish to go. Remember, this is a judgment-free zone. The goal here isn't to get a perfect score but to gain a better understanding of your emotional landscape. There are no "right" or "wrong" answers—only insights that will help you grow.

Evaluating Emotional Triggers: The Trigger Journal

As we explored in Chapter 2, understanding your emotional triggers is the first step in navigating conflicts effectively. To help you dig a little deeper into your own triggers, we're introducing the 'Trigger Journal.'

For the next week, carry a small notebook or use an app on your phone to jot down moments when you feel a strong emotional reaction. It could be irritation at a colleague's comment, anxiety from an unexpected bill, or even joy from a child's hug. Don't overthink it—just note it down.

Doing this may not only unearth patterns but also help you become more self-aware in the heat of the moment. By the end of the week, you'll have a candid snapshot of your emotional responses, providing you a starting point for deeper reflection.

Pattern Recognition

After a week of diligently maintaining your Trigger Journal, you'll likely have a treasure trove of emotional data at your fingertips. Now comes the illuminating part—pattern recognition. You see, emotions aren't random; they often follow a pattern, like clues leading us to the root of a recurring issue.

So, take your Trigger Journal and cast a discerning eye over your entries. Do you find that you're mostly triggered by a specific person? If so, what does that reveal about the dynamics of that relationship? Or perhaps it's a particular setting that gets your emotional alarms ringing—like work meetings or family dinners. Could it be the atmosphere, or maybe the topics that are usually discussed?

And let's not forget timing. Do your triggers seem to activate more in the mornings when you're just gearing up for the day, or in the evenings when you're winding down? Understanding the 'when' can give us significant clues about the 'why.'

Remember, the aim isn't to judge yourself but to understand your emotional landscape better. Because in that understanding, you'll find the keys to managing your triggers more effectively.

Reflection Questions

As you review your Trigger Journal and the patterns you've identified, it's valuable to engage in deeper reflection. This is your chance to peel back the layers, to ask yourself the 'why' behind the 'what.'

- What emotions are you most likely to feel during a conflict?** Is it anger, frustration, or perhaps sadness? Understanding your go-to emotions can reveal a lot about your emotional coping mechanisms.
- Can you identify underlying fears or insecurities that these triggers might be pointing to?** For instance, if you're often triggered by feeling ignored, could that connect to a deeper fear of abandonment or being overlooked?

Reflecting on these questions isn't just an intellectual exercise; it's emotional spelunking. You're diving deep into your emotional caverns to discover the hidden gems that illuminate your behavioral patterns. Take your time with this. You might even want to jot down your reflections in your Trigger Journal for a more comprehensive view.

Assessing Empathy Levels

Now that we've taken a deep dive into your emotional triggers, let's shift our focus to your capacity for empathy. Consider the following hypothetical conflict scenarios and jot down how you'd respond. Aim to approach each situation with empathy in mind. Would you actively listen? Would you try to put yourself in the other person's shoes?

These scenarios aren't just thought exercises; they're rehearsal stages for real life. By practicing empathic responses, you're not only honing your skills but also preparing for future conflicts that inevitably arise.

Certainly, let's dive into these scenarios designed to challenge and expand your empathic skills:

- Family Dinner Fallout: Imagine you're at a family dinner and a heated argument erupts between two relatives over politics. Tensions are high, and everyone is choosing sides. What would your empathic response be?
- Workplace Woes: You notice a colleague is consistently late with their part of a project, causing stress for the team. You're tempted to call them out during a team meeting. How would you handle the situation empathically?
- Friendship Friction: Your close friend has been distant lately and finally admits they're going through a tough time but aren't ready to talk about it yet. How do you respond with empathy while respecting their boundaries?
- Social Media Showdown: You come across a post that strongly opposes your beliefs, and you feel the urge to comment. What would an empathic response look like in this digital landscape?

These scenarios are designed to stretch your empathic muscles and challenge your default reactions. Take your time to write down your responses, focusing on how empathy can serve as a guiding light in each situation.

Self Assessment

Absolutely, let's dive into a self-assessment exercise. This questionnaire is a tool for introspection, a mirror to better understand your current level of empathy. Answer the following questions honestly, rating yourself on a scale from 1 (Never) to 5 (Always):

1. Listening Skills: Do you actively listen when someone is talking to you, without interrupting or formulating your response while they're speaking?
2. Emotional Awareness: Can you usually identify what emotions others are feeling based on their expressions, tone of voice, or body language?
3. Non-Judgment: Do you find it easy to withhold judgment when someone shares a different perspective or makes a choice you don't agree with?
4. Comfort with Silence: Are you comfortable with moments of silence in a conversation, recognizing it as a space for reflection rather than something to be filled?
5. Curiosity: Do you ask follow-up questions to better understand someone's feelings or perspective?
6. Vulnerability: Are you willing to share your own emotions and vulnerabilities in a conversation to foster a deeper connection?
7. Validation: Do you make an effort to validate other people's feelings, even if you don't fully understand them?
8. Willingness to Help: Do you often find yourself considering ways to help someone who's struggling, whether it's offering emotional support or taking action?

Add up your scores to get a total. This number isn't a definitive measure of your empathy, but it can serve as a useful indicator of where you might focus your efforts in cultivating more empathic skills. As you work on your empathy take this questionnaire periodically to see how you've grown.

Self Reflection Questions

Reflection questions serve as mental signposts, inviting you to pause and consider your own journey in the realm of empathy. Here are a few questions to ponder:

1. Can you recall a recent situation where you could have been more empathic? What held you back?
2. Have you ever caught yourself judging someone too quickly in a conflict situation? What assumptions did you make?
3. Think of a time when someone showed you great empathy. How did it make you feel, and what impact did it have on the situation?
4. Are there certain people or situations where you find it easier to be empathic? Why do you think that is?
5. If you scored lower on any aspect of the self-assessment, what actionable steps can you take to improve?
6. How does your level of empathy change when you are stressed or overwhelmed? Are there strategies you could employ to maintain empathy even in high-stress situations?

These questions are intended to deepen your understanding and awareness of your own empathic abilities. They can be revisited time and again as you progress through your journey toward becoming a more empathic individual. Take some time to journal your answers or simply reflect on them mentally.

As we close this reflective interlude, it's crucial to think of it not as an endpoint, but as a launching pad for your ongoing journey of emotional and empathic growth. You've just taken some significant steps in understanding your emotional triggers and assessing your levels of empathy. But remember, self-awareness is a practice, not a destination.

Next Steps for Your Journey

- Revisit the Exercises: Once you've completed the entire book, come back to this interlude. You'll likely find that your answers and perspectives have evolved, offering a valuable measure of your growth.
- Daily Reflection: Take a few minutes at the end of each day to reflect on your emotional experiences. Did you recognize any of your triggers? Were you able to employ empathy in a challenging situation?
- Seek Feedback: Don't shy away from asking close friends or family members for their insights on your emotional intelligence and

empathic skills. Sometimes, an external perspective can provide invaluable insights.

- Read Widely: There are a plethora of excellent books and articles on emotional intelligence and empathy. Diversifying your reading can offer you new tools and perspectives.

- Mindfulness and Active Listening: These are practical skills that can significantly boost your emotional intelligence. Consider adopting a simple daily mindfulness practice and actively focus on improving your listening skills in conversations.

- Professional Guidance: If you find that emotional triggers or a lack of empathy are significantly impacting your life, it may be helpful to seek the guidance of a trained therapist or counselor.

As you close this chapter and set this book aside for a moment, consider this: What one actionable step will you commit to today to improve your emotional intelligence and empathy? Remember, the journey of a thousand miles begins with a single step.

Stay tuned, because in Part II, we'll go even deeper into the practical tools and frameworks that will enable you to transform conflicts into opportunities for connection. Are you ready to take the next step?

PART TWO
The Toolbox

Chapter 4: The "Seek First to Understand" Principle

"The most basic of all human needs is the need to understand and be understood. The best way to understand people is to listen to them."

– Ralph G. Nichols

Welcome to Part II of our journey—the part where we roll up our sleeves and get our hands dirty with the practical tools that can transform our conflicts into opportunities for growth. And what better place to start than with a principle that epitomizes the essence of constructive conversations: "Seek First to Understand, Then to be Understood."

This mantra, borrowed from Stephen Covey's renowned book, "The 7 Habits of Highly Effective People," is a game-changer in the realm of human interactions. Think of it as your Swiss Army knife in the wilderness of conflict—a multi-tool designed to help you navigate through the thicket of emotions, judgments, and misunderstandings that make conflicts so daunting.

In this chapter, we'll dissect this principle, explore its application in conflict situations, and arm you with actionable steps for implementation. By the end of this chapter, you won't just understand the "Seek First to Understand" principle; you'll know how to apply it in the crucible of your daily conflicts.

Ready? Let's dive in.

Deep Dive into Stephen Covey's Principle

The "Seek First to Understand, Then to be Understood" principle finds its roots in Stephen Covey's seminal work, "The 7 Habits of Highly Effective People." This book, a cornerstone in personal development literature, presents seven habits that serve as building blocks for a fulfilling life. And nestled within these habits is the one we're spotlighting today—a habit that challenges us to shift our communication paradigm.

In a world where the majority of our conversations consist of us waiting for our turn to speak, this principle turns the tables. It urges us to engage in empathic listening, a form of listening that goes beyond merely hearing words. Empathic listening requires us to tune into the emotional undertones, the unspoken needs, and the hidden agendas that often lurk behind the spoken word. It asks us to set aside our judgments and truly step into the shoes of the other person, if only for a moment.

Think of it this way: how often have you found yourself in a heated discussion, only to realize you've been formulating your next argument rather than actually listening? It's a common pitfall. But this habit teaches us to flip the script. It guides us to listen with the intent to understand, not merely to reply.

By adopting this approach, we don't just become better communicators; we become better partners, friends, and community members. Empathic listening becomes a bridge to effective communication, one that allows us to transform the very nature of our interactions and, consequently, our conflicts.

Let's peel back the layers of this transformative principle, shall we?

Listening: The Gateway to Understanding

The first layer, listening, may appear straightforward but is often the most overlooked. We hear, but do we truly listen? Genuine listening is an active process that requires full attention, not just an idle activity we engage in while awaiting our chance to speak. It means turning off our internal chatter and truly hearing the words, the tone, and even the silence between the words.

Listening is also about letting go of preconceived notions and judgments. It's about creating a space where the other person feels seen and heard. This is your time to gather data, to collect the pieces of the puzzle that will later help you understand the bigger picture. Have you ever noticed how a single clarifying question can turn the tide in a conversation? That's the power of active listening.

Understanding: The Heart of the Matter

The second layer, understanding, is what we aim to achieve through our attentive listening. But understanding goes beyond just comprehending the words being said. It's about grasping the emotions, motivations, and concerns behind those words. It's the moment when you say, "I get where you're coming from," and genuinely mean it.

Understanding is also where empathy plays a crucial role. It allows us to see the issue from the other person's perspective, even if we don't necessarily agree with it. Isn't it liberating to realize that understanding someone doesn't mean you have to forsake your own beliefs? It's a middle ground where mutual respect can flourish.

Speaking: The Culmination of Listen and Understand

Finally, we arrive at speaking, the third layer. This is where you articulate your own perspective, but it's framed by the rich understanding you've gained from the first two layers. By this point, your words are not just reactive responses or canned arguments; they're thoughtful expressions aimed at reaching a shared understanding.

Here's the clincher: When you speak from a place of understanding, your words carry a different kind of weight. They're infused with a sincerity that's palpable, and it's this sincerity that often diffuses tension and invites open dialogue. Ever notice how a well-timed acknowledgment can defuse a heated situation? That's speaking backed by listening and understanding.

The Golden Rule Reimagined

We're all familiar with the Golden Rule: "Do unto others as you would have them do unto you." It's a principle that transcends cultural, religious, and ethical boundaries, urging us to treat others with kindness and respect. But what Stephen Covey's principle of "Seek First to Understand, Then to Be Understood" does is to add a layer of nuance to this age-old rule.

The Golden Rule assumes, to some extent, a level of self-awareness and self-centeredness. "I know how I want to be treated, so I'll treat you the same way." Yet, what if the way you wish to be treated isn't the same as the other person? Enter Covey's principle, which nudges us to first understand the unique needs, desires, and perspectives of the other person before we act or speak. It's like saying, "Let me understand how you want to be treated, and then I'll do my best to treat you that way."

In conflicts, this is groundbreaking. We often rush to solve problems based on our own frame of reference. We think, "If it were me, I'd want..." and proceed accordingly. Covey's principle forces us to pause, to listen and understand the other side before taking any action or even forming a response. It's the Golden Rule but with a set of empathetic headphones on. The focus shifts from "doing" to "understanding," making it less about immediate action and more about thoughtful interaction.

By doing so, this principle elevates the Golden Rule from a guideline for ethical conduct to a dynamic tool for navigating complex human interactions. Wouldn't you agree that this adds a whole new layer of sophistication to the way we handle conflicts?

The Listening Gap: The Silent Culprit in Escalating Conflicts

Picture this: you're in a heated discussion, maybe with a partner or a colleague. The room's atmosphere is thick with tension, and words are flying like arrows in a battlefield. Now pause and ask yourself, "How much am I actually hearing?" Chances are, not much. The irony of conflict situations is that while they demand nuanced understanding more than ever, they often turn into a cacophony where everyone is eager to be heard but reluctant to listen. We're all busy formulating our next counterargument, our next line of defense, or our next accusation. The result? A widening chasm of misunderstanding, with both sides feeling unheard and unacknowledged.

Stephen Covey's principle of "Seek First to Understand, Then to Be Understood" swoops in as a much-needed antidote to this listening gap. It urges us to flip the script; to halt our internal monologue just long enough to tune into the other person's frequency. It's not about surrendering your viewpoint or stifling your voice. Instead, it's about making a conscious effort to understand the other person's perspective fully before voicing your own.

This approach does something magical: it defuses tension. When people feel heard, their defensive walls start to crumble. Their tone softens, and their willingness to find common ground increases. The principle doesn't just promote effective communication; it cultivates a richer, more nuanced form of dialogue that goes beyond mere transactional exchanges. It turns what could be a zero-sum game into a win-win scenario.

Imagine how much we could resolve by simply mastering this art of attentive listening. It's not just a courtesy; it's a lifeline in our discourse, a bridge over troubled interpersonal waters. Wouldn't you say it's high time we close this listening gap?

Breaking Down Walls: The Transformative Power of Understanding

Conflict can often feel like two fortresses facing each other, with moats full of misunderstandings and walls built from hardened perspectives. Both sides are heavily guarded, cannons aimed, and flags hoisted. But what if I told you that the most powerful tool in your arsenal isn't a weapon but a pair of open ears?

Taking the time to genuinely understand the other person does something remarkable: it dissolves barriers. It's akin to lowering your drawbridge and inviting the "enemy" in for a diplomatic conversation over a cup of tea. The more you listen, the more you understand, and the more you understand, the easier it becomes to find a path towards resolution.

Understanding someone else's viewpoint does not mean you have to agree with it. You don't have to dismantle your own fortress or renounce your values. Rather, it's about recognizing that the other person's perspective is built from their unique life experiences, just as yours is. When you approach conflicts with the aim to understand before being understood, you're not just hearing words. You're listening to the chapters in their life story that led them to feel this way. You're acknowledging the emotions, fears, and hopes that underpin their arguments.

By breaking down these metaphorical walls, you're creating a space where constructive conversation can flourish. It's a space where defenses are lowered, trust is built, and both parties are more open to finding that elusive middle ground. Isn't that a place where you'd rather be?

Real Life Examples

Let's dive into some real-life examples that illuminate how the "Seek First to Understand" principle has turned conflicts into springboards for growth and deeper connections.

Case Study 1: The Corporate Boardroom

In a high-stakes corporate boardroom, the atmosphere was electric. Two senior executives, Laura and Ahmed, were at loggerheads over the direction of a new product launch. Laura advocated for a fast rollout to capitalize on market trends, while Ahmed insisted on a more cautious, research-driven approach.

Ahmed took a deep breath and decided to apply the principle of seeking first to understand. Instead of pushing his agenda, he asked Laura to elaborate on her reasoning. As Laura spoke, Ahmed listened intently, even jotting down notes. The room's temperature seemed to drop a few degrees.

By genuinely listening to Laura, Ahmed discovered a crucial piece of information: Laura had insights into consumer behavior that he hadn't considered. In turn, Laura felt heard and was more open to Ahmed's concerns about potential risks. The result? A hybrid strategy that combined both their strengths, a successful product launch, and two executives who now had a deep-rooted respect for each other's expertise.

Case Study 2: A Marriage on the Brink

Sarah and Mark had reached a breaking point in their marriage. The issue? Work-life balance. Sarah felt neglected as Mark was always working late, while Mark felt pressured and misunderstood.

Instead of filing for divorce papers, they chose to seek couples therapy. The therapist introduced them to the principle of "Seek First to Understand." During one session, Sarah shared her fears and insecurities, and for the first time, Mark didn't interrupt or get defensive. He listened.

Suddenly, Mark understood the loneliness Sarah felt, and Sarah understood the enormous stress Mark was under at work. This newfound understanding didn't solve all their problems overnight, but it was a turning point. They started to work together to find a balance, which eventually led to a more harmonious life and a marriage that was saved.

Case Study 3: The Neighborhood Feud

Two neighbors, Emily and Raj, had a long-standing feud over a tree that was causing shade in Emily's yard. Community meetings turned hostile, and legal action was on the horizon. One day, Raj invited Emily over for coffee and applied the "Seek First to Understand" principle. He listened to Emily's concerns without interjecting his own counter-arguments.

What happened next was nothing short of miraculous. Emily acknowledged that the tree held sentimental value for Raj's family, and Raj understood Emily's concerns about her garden's well-being. They reached a compromise to trim the branches rather than cutting the tree down. Their relationship transformed from hostile neighbors to friends.

Daily Implemtation

We've laid the theoretical groundwork and seen the transformative power of Stephen Covey's "Seek First to Understand" principle in action. Now, it's time to roll up our sleeves and dive into the practical tools and techniques that can make this principle a living, breathing part of your daily interactions. Whether it's a casual conversation or a heated debate, these actionable steps are designed to equip you with the skills to navigate conflicts constructively. Ready to get hands-on? Let's dive in.

Active Listening

Active listening isn't just about being quiet while the other person talks; it's about giving them your full attention and showing that you're engaged. It's the difference between hearing and truly listening. So, how do you demonstrate that you're actively listening, especially in the throes of a disagreement where emotions run high? Let's explore some tried-and-true techniques.

Paraphrasing

Imagine you're having a disagreement about household chores. Your partner says, "I feel like I'm doing all the work around here, and it's draining me." Instead of getting defensive, you could respond with, "So you're feeling overwhelmed because you think the chores aren't equally distributed, is that right?" By paraphrasing, you're showing that you've heard them and are trying to understand their point of view.

Nodding

Sometimes, non-verbal cues speak volumes. A simple nod can go a long way in showing that you're engaged and attentive. However, don't overdo it; your aim is to look interested, not like a bobblehead.

Asking Open-Ended Questions

Open-ended questions are a golden ticket to deeper understanding. Instead of asking questions that can be answered with a simple 'yes' or 'no,' pose queries that require a more elaborative response. In the middle of a disagreement about weekend plans, you could ask, "What's making this weekend so important to you?" This not only shows that you're listening but also invites the other person to share more of their perspective.

By integrating these active listening techniques into your interactions, you're not just showing courtesy; you're laying the foundation for a more empathic and meaningful dialogue. Remember, in the landscape of conflict, listening is not a passive act but a powerful tool for transformation.

The Art of the Pause

Ah, the art of the pause—a seemingly simple act that holds immense power, especially in the context of a conflict. Picture this: you're in a heated discussion, and you feel the urge to immediately counter the other person's argument. It's a natural instinct, right? We often fear that pausing will make us appear weak or unsure. But what if I told you that this impulse to rush into a response is often counterproductive?

When you pause, you create a momentary space, a kind of emotional and cognitive "breathing room." This brief interlude allows you to process what's just been said. Did you truly understand the point the other person was making? Could there be layers or nuances that escaped you in the heat of the moment? A pause lets you mull over these questions.

Moreover, pausing gives you the opportunity to formulate a more measured and thoughtful response. Let's say a coworker criticizes your project. Your immediate reaction might be defensive. But a pause allows you to consider whether there's merit in their critique. Maybe they've seen an issue you've missed. Responding thoughtfully not only shows maturity but can also enhance the quality of your work.

So, how do you master this art? One technique is the "three-breath rule." Whenever you feel the urge to jump in with a response, take three deep breaths. Use this time to reflect on what's been said and how you want to respond. Another method is to mentally count to five. Believe it or not, those few seconds can make a world of difference in the quality of your interactions.

The art of the pause is like a secret weapon in your conversational toolkit. It's not about hesitating or showing uncertainty; it's about exercising control over your reactions. Think of it as a soft but sturdy buffer that prevents minor disagreements from escalating into full-blown conflicts.

Are you willing to experiment with this technique in your next contentious discussion? How might the dynamic change if you allowed yourself the grace of a pause?

In the swirling currents of a conflict, there's a buoy that can help both parties find their footing—empathic validation. It's a concept that's deceptively simple yet incredibly potent. Empathic validation involves recognizing and affirming the other person's emotions or perspective. It doesn't mean you agree with what they're saying or how they're feeling; rather, you're acknowledging their experience as valid for them.

Empathic Validation

Imagine you're having a disagreement with a friend who feels overlooked in your relationship. You might think you've been a good friend, but instead of immediately defending yourself, you say, "I hear you. It sounds like you're feeling neglected, and that's not what I want for our friendship." This simple act of validating their feelings can work wonders. Why? Because most people in conflict aren't just seeking a solution; they're seeking to be heard and understood.

Empathic validation essentially says, "I see you. I hear you. What you're experiencing matters to me." This form of acknowledgment can defuse the emotional charge in a conflict and pave the way for a more rational, constructive dialogue. You're not conceding your stance; rather, you're demonstrating that you value the other person's experience.

Now, you might be wondering, "How can I validate someone's perspective if I fundamentally disagree?" The key lies in separating the person from the viewpoint. You can disagree with someone's opinion while still respecting their right to hold it. Phrases like "I can see how you'd feel that way" or "I understand that this is important to you" can go a long way in fostering a climate of mutual respect.

When you practice empathic validation, you're not just diffusing tension; you're also inviting a deeper level of conversation. The other person is more likely to lower their defenses, listen to you in return, and consider alternative perspectives. This can lead to more constructive solutions and, ultimately, a stronger, more empathic relationship.

So, how might empathic validation change the dynamics of your next disagreement? Are you willing to set aside your immediate judgments and just listen?

The "Three Open Questions" Exercise: A Compass for Navigating Conflict

In the labyrinth of conflict, it's easy to lose your way. The "Three Open Questions" exercise serves as a navigational tool to help you explore the terrain of the other person's perspective. The idea is straightforward yet impactful: During your next disagreement, challenge yourself to ask three open-ended questions. These aren't just any questions; they're designed to dig deeper into the soil of the other person's viewpoint, to unearth the roots of their stance.

Open-ended questions are like keys that unlock hidden doors. Unlike yes-or-no questions, which often act like stop signs in a conversation, open-ended questions invite elaboration. They say, "Tell me more," encouraging the other person to share their thoughts, feelings, and motivations.

Crafting Your Questions
- Understanding the Emotion: Start with a question that seeks to understand the emotional core of the other person's viewpoint. For example, "How did that situation make you feel?"
- Exploring the Reasoning: Next, ask a question that dives into the logic or values behind their stance. You could ask, "What experiences or beliefs are informing your perspective?"

- Vision for Resolution: Finally, encourage forward-thinking with a question about solutions or outcomes. For example, "What would an ideal resolution look like for you?"

The Payoff

By asking these three open-ended questions, you're doing several things simultaneously. First, you're showing that you're genuinely interested in understanding the other person. Second, you're gathering valuable information that can guide the conversation toward a mutually satisfying resolution. Lastly, you're creating an environment where constructive, respectful dialogue can flourish.

So, what would happen if you incorporated this exercise into your conflict resolution toolkit? Could it be the game-changer you've been searching for?

Wrapping Up Chapter 4: Turning Principle into Practice

As we come to the end of this enlightening chapter, let's take a moment to gather the insights we've collected along the way. We've journeyed through the wisdom of Stephen Covey's "Seek First to Understand, Then to Be Understood" principle, dissecting it into its vital components—listening, understanding, and speaking. We've seen how it acts as an evolved version of the Golden Rule, tuned specifically for conflict resolution.

We also explored its transformative power in real-world conflicts. It's not just a theoretical concept but a practical guide that fills the often-overlooked "listening gap" and tears down the barriers that hamper genuine dialogue. Through case studies, we glimpsed how the principle can turn seemingly insurmountable conflicts into opportunities for growth and connection.

Finally, we ventured into actionable territory. From active listening techniques to the art of the pause, we've equipped you with a set of tools designed to make the principle a living, breathing part of your daily interactions. The "Three Open Questions" exercise serves as a practical rehearsal space for you to apply this wisdom in real-time.

As we close this chapter, consider this: the shift from understanding the "what" and "why" to mastering the "how" of constructive conversations has been significant. You're not just a spectator anymore; you're an active participant in your own story and the stories of those around you. The stage is set, the tools are in hand; are you ready to rewrite the script of your conflicts?

Pit Stop for Reflection: Pause, Ponder, Practice

Before we forge ahead, let's take a brief but meaningful pit stop. It's a chance to switch from absorbing new information to reflecting on your own experiences and challenges. Grab a notebook or simply take a mental inventory as we explore these questions:

1. Have you ever tried to apply the "Seek First to Understand" principle in a conflict? What was the outcome? Perhaps it's a recent disagreement with a loved one or a long-standing issue at work. Reflect on whether you've consciously or unconsciously applied this principle. Did it change the trajectory of the conversation? Did it lead to a more satisfying resolution for all parties involved?

2. What are some barriers you've encountered when trying to listen actively during a disagreement? Is it impatience, the urge to interrupt, or perhaps a preconceived notion about the other person's motives? Dig deep and try to identify those roadblocks that have kept you from fully embracing the act of empathic listening.

This pit stop is more than a mere break; it's an integral part of your journey towards mastering the art of constructive conversations. So, give yourself the time and space to ponder these questions. You might find that the answers not only deepen your understanding of the material we've covered but also illuminate the path for the chapters ahead.

Ready to move on? The next leg of our journey promises to be just as enriching. Shall we?

Chapter 5: Creating a 'Safe Space'

"True dialogue cannot exist unless each of us crosses the boundary of our own self and enters the unfamiliar territory of another."

– Harville Hendrix

Welcome to Chapter 5, a pivotal juncture in our journey. Imagine your conversations as rooms—some feel like comforting living rooms where you can kick off your shoes, while others feel more like interrogation chambers. The difference often boils down to one crucial factor: psychological safety. In this chapter, we'll explore what it means to construct a 'safe space' for dialogue, why it's so transformative, and how to practically build it, brick by emotional brick.

We'll examine the research that underscores the importance of psychological safety and look into its symbiotic relationship with trust. We'll also explore how a safe space allows vulnerability and openness to flourish, enriching not just individual conversations but potentially the entire climate of a relationship or organization.

And because knowing is only half the battle, we'll provide you with concrete strategies—from establishing ground rules to understanding non-verbal cues—to make these safe spaces a reality.

So, are you ready to become the architect of your own conversational environments? Let's lay the first stone.

The Theory and Practice of Psychological Safety

Psychological safety is the invisible yet palpable boundary that defines the quality of our interactions. In the realm of conversation, think of it as an emotionally padded room where the walls are built with understanding, respect, and freedom. Here, you can speak your mind, ask questions, or express dissent, all without the looming cloud of judgment or the risk of punitive action. It's a space where your voice doesn't waver, and your words aren't sifted through a sieve of fear or apprehension.

Why is this so transformative? Because a psychologically safe space liberates the best in us—it allows for the expression of authentic thoughts, candid feedback, and creative ideas. It turns the spotlight away from the risks of humiliation or failure and refocuses it on constructive dialogue and collaborative problem-solving. Would you agree that this is a setting most of us would want to converse in?

The Research Behind Psychological Safety

You might be wondering, is this concept of psychological safety just feel-good jargon, or is there substance behind it? There's ample research to affirm its importance, particularly in team dynamics and interpersonal relationships. In fact, Google's Project Aristotle, which aimed to discover what makes a team effective, found that psychological safety was the number-one factor. Teams that exhibited high levels of psychological safety outperformed those that didn't, both in terms of productivity and overall well-being.

Moreover, studies in social psychology reveal that psychological safety plays a pivotal role in how we form and maintain relationships. When people feel safe, they are more willing to take interpersonal risks, like sharing personal experiences or expressing unpopular opinions. And these risks? They're the bedrock of deep, meaningful relationships. Think about it—wouldn't you be more inclined to share your thoughts and feelings in a space where you're assured of empathic listening and non-judgmental responses?

This isn't just academic musings; it's a science-backed cornerstone for building effective teams and nurturing lasting relationships.

The Trust Factor: The Symbiotic Relationship Between Psychological Safety and Trust

Imagine you're standing on the edge of a diving board, contemplating whether to jump into the pool below. What's the deciding factor? Trust. Trust that the water will support you, and trust in your ability to swim. Similarly, trust is the underpinning factor when we decide to open up in a conversation, to take the metaphorical plunge into vulnerability.

Psychological safety and trust share an intricate, symbiotic relationship. When a conversational space is psychologically safe, it acts like fertile soil where the seed of trust can be planted and nurtured. In this environment, people are willing to be themselves, to share their thoughts, feelings, and even doubts, without the looming cloud of judgment or reprisal. Once you've experienced this level of safety with someone, doesn't your trust in them grow? You think, "Here's a person with whom I can be my authentic self."

But here's the beautiful part: as trust grows, it fortifies that sense of psychological safety. When you trust someone, you're more inclined to give them the benefit of the doubt, to interpret their words and actions in a positive light. This creates a virtuous cycle: trust enhances safety, and safety, in turn, deepens trust. It's akin to a dance where each partner moves in sync, instinctively knowing when to take a step forward or when to pause.

Think about your own relationships for a moment. Can you identify situations where an initial sense of safety led to a deeper level of trust? And how did that trust further enhance your sense of safety in that relationship? It's a dance you've likely been part of, perhaps without even realizing it.

The Vulnerability Paradox: The Unexpected Strength of Revealing Your Soft Underbelly

Picture an oyster. Protected by a hard shell, it keeps its soft interior hidden away. Yet, it's precisely this vulnerable part, this soft underbelly, that produces the pearl. The oyster, in its vulnerability, creates something beautiful and treasured. Now, let's translate this to human interactions. Often, we build emotional "shells" to protect ourselves, especially in conflicts. But what if we dared to open up, to show our vulnerable side? What kind of pearls might we produce in our relationships?

There's a pervasive myth that vulnerability equals weakness. In reality, it's the opposite. Vulnerability is an act of courage; it's showing up and allowing yourself to be seen, warts and all. When you let down your guard in a psychologically safe space, you're not just saying, "This is me." You're also extending an unspoken invitation to the other person: "I trust you enough to show you my true self. Will you do the same?"

And here's where the paradox comes alive. By showing vulnerability, you're not handing the other person a weapon to use against you; more often than not, you're handing them a tool of connection. This act deepens emotional bonds and fosters trust. It communicates that you're not just interested in winning an argument but are invested in the relationship itself. Vulnerability opens the door to a more honest, more authentic, and more empathetic form of interaction.

Ever found yourself in a situation where someone opened up to you, and you felt compelled to reciprocate? That's vulnerability fostering openness, acting like a mirror. The more open you are, the more it invites the other person to shed their own protective layers.

Openness as a Two-Way Street: The Symbiotic Dance of Authenticity

Imagine a two-lane road. Traffic flows in both directions, each lane influencing the other. If one lane gets blocked, the entire road feels the impact. Openness in a conversation operates much the same way—it's a two-way street.

When you create a safe space, you're not just making room for your own openness; you're paving the way for the other person to be open, too. It's a symbiotic relationship. Your willingness to be transparent can set the tone for the entire conversation. It's like lighting a single candle in a dark room. That small flame can inspire another person to light their candle, and soon enough, the room is filled with light.

Let's not underestimate the power of this mutual openness. In conflict situations, it can be transformative. Imagine you're in a heated debate with a friend about a sensitive issue. You decide to be the first to lower your guard, sharing a personal story that illustrates your perspective. The atmosphere shifts, almost palpably. Your friend pauses, takes a deep breath, and begins to share their own story. Suddenly, the conversation isn't just an exchange of arguments; it's an exchange of experiences, of pieces of your lives. The dynamic changes from one of opposition to one of mutual exploration.

Being open invites openness. It turns the conversation from a battlefield into a meeting ground, from a problem to be solved into an experience to be shared. This kind of mutual openness doesn't just resolve conflicts; it transforms them into opportunities for deeper connection.

So, can you recall a time when your openness encouraged someone else to be more open? What happened? How did it feel to experience that mutual vulnerability?

The Ripple Effect: Changing the Course One Conversation at a Time

Picture a pond, still and calm. Now imagine tossing a stone into it. The stone creates a splash, but the impact doesn't stop there. Ripples extend outward, reaching far corners of the pond that the stone never touched. One safe and open conversation can have a similar ripple effect on the dynamics of a relationship or a team setting.

Let's say you're at work, and there's been an ongoing tension within your team. You decide to have an open and honest discussion with a colleague about the issues at hand. You both approach the conversation with a commitment to psychological safety. Words are measured, tones are even, and at the end, you both leave feeling like you've been heard. That's one ripple.

Now, what happens next? You both carry that experience into your next team meeting. You find that your interactions are less guarded, more constructive. That's another ripple. Other team members start to notice this subtle change in dynamics, and they, too, begin to drop their guards. More ripples. Before you know it, the overall tone of the team starts to shift from one of tension to one of collaborative problem-solving.

The ripple effect also applies in personal relationships. Perhaps you have a family member you've always struggled to communicate with. One good, open conversation could be the stepping stone to a healthier, more communicative relationship moving forward. It sets a precedent, a new norm that says, "This is how we can interact when we respect each other's perspectives."

It's important to note that ripples can take time to spread and may require more than one "stone" to effect substantial change. However, never underestimate the power of a single positive interaction to set a new course for future conversations.

Ground Rules: Laying the Foundation for Safe Dialogue

Imagine stepping onto a basketball court. The lines, the hoops, the rules—they all create a space where the game can unfold in an organized manner. Similarly, establishing ground rules at the beginning of a difficult conversation creates a safe "court" where both participants can engage without stepping out of bounds.

Ground rules act like traffic signals. They control the flow of the conversation, making sure everyone gets a fair chance to move ahead. Simple rules like "no interruptions" or "confirming understanding before moving on to a new point" can go a long way in preventing conversational pile-ups.

These rules are not just formalities; they're an investment in the quality of the dialogue. By setting these parameters, you're making a mutual commitment to respect and understanding, making it easier to navigate tricky emotional terrain.

Imagine you're about to discuss a sensitive topic with a friend. You could start by saying, "Can we agree to let each other finish speaking before responding?" or "How about we clarify what we mean if there's any confusion, rather than making assumptions?" This sets the tone for a constructive and respectful exchange.

What's important is that these ground rules are agreed upon by both parties. This creates a level playing field and adds an element of fairness to the conversation. And remember, the objective isn't to win; it's to understand and to be understood.

Wouldn't it be liberating to know that you're entering a conversation where the chances of misunderstanding or escalation are minimized? Ground rules can offer that assurance.

Non-Verbal Cues: The Unspoken Language of Safety

You walk into a room and someone glances at you with a warm smile. Instantly, you feel a sense of welcome, don't you? This illustrates the power of non-verbal cues in shaping the atmosphere of a conversation. It's not just what you say, but how you say it—and that includes body language.

In a conversation, eye contact can work like a spotlight, focusing your attention on the other person. It sends a message: "I see you, and I'm listening." Nodding, meanwhile, functions like a reassuring pat on the back. It doesn't necessarily mean agreement, but it does signify understanding or acknowledgment.

Open postures—such as uncrossed arms or leaning slightly forward—can act like an invitation, saying, "I'm open to what you have to say." These gestures contribute to creating a safe space, much like soft lighting makes a room feel cozy and inviting.

Think about it this way: Your body language is like the background music in a movie scene. It sets the tone and influences the emotional climate. Sure, you could have a meaningful conversation in complete silence, but a well-chosen soundtrack enhances the experience, doesn't it?

So, in your next challenging conversation, be mindful of your non-verbal cues. They're not just garnishes; they're key ingredients that can either spice up or spoil the dialogical feast you're sharing with someone.

The "Pause and Reflect" Technique: The Power of a Well-Timed Pause

Imagine you're listening to a symphony. The beauty isn't just in the notes but also in the pauses between them. Similarly, a conversation can become a harmonious exchange when punctuated by meaningful pauses. The "Pause and Reflect" technique serves as a valuable tool in cultivating a safe conversational space.

So, what is the "Pause and Reflect" technique? Simply put, it's about intentionally taking turns to speak, separated by short pauses for reflection and clarification. Picture this: You've just heard the other person make a point. Instead of jumping in with your response, you pause. You give yourself a moment to digest what's been said. Then, you reflect back your understanding, perhaps by saying, "So, if I'm hearing you right, you're saying..." This ensures that you've not only heard but understood the other person's viewpoint.

The pause does something else, too. It gives you the space to breathe, to collect your thoughts, and to formulate a response that aligns with your understanding and feelings. It's like taking a sip of water during a marathon; it refreshes and re-energizes you for the next leg of the journey.

By practicing this technique, you create a rhythm in the conversation. You invite an ebb and flow that makes the exchange more balanced, more equitable, and yes, safer. So, the next time you find yourself in a heated discussion, remember: Pause and Reflect. It's not a sign of hesitance but a hallmark of thoughtful communication.

Conflict Resolution Styles Inventory: The Compass for Navigating Conversations

Life is an array of choices, and the way we handle conflicts is no exception. Understanding not just your own but also others' preferred styles of conflict resolution can be a game-changer in creating a psychologically safe environment.

Think of it like this: If conversations are journeys, then knowing your conflict resolution style is like having a compass. Whether you're the type to confront issues head-on (akin to a "north" orientation on the compass) or someone who prefers to avoid conflict (perhaps a "south" orientation), recognizing these tendencies is the first step toward navigating conversations more effectively.

Here's a brief exercise to help you get a grip on your conflict resolution style:

- The Confronter: Do you tend to directly address issues as they arise?
- The Avoider: Do you sidestep conflicts, hoping they'll resolve themselves?
- The Compromiser: Are you willing to give a little to get a little?
- The Collaborator: Do you seek a win-win solution that satisfies both parties?
- The Accommodator: Are you inclined to put others' needs before your own to maintain harmony?

Rate yourself on a scale of 1-5 for each style, with 1 being "rarely me" and 5 being "this is so me."

Now, consider doing this exercise with your frequent conversational partners, or even as a team exercise in a professional setting. It's eye-opening to see how different styles can either clash or harmonize, isn't it? By identifying these styles, you can tailor your approach, enabling a smoother, safer dialogue for all involved.

Wrapping Up Chapter 5: Your Blueprint for a Safe Space

We've journeyed through the landscapes of psychological safety, vulnerability, and the art of cultivating a nurturing conversational environment. The principles and guidelines we've discussed are not just theoretical constructs; they are your blueprint for creating safe spaces where meaningful dialogue can occur. From understanding the bedrock of trust to recognizing the ripple effects of one open conversation, we've laid out a comprehensive roadmap.

Think of this chapter as your 'Architect's Toolkit' for dialogues. Just as an architect wouldn't build a house without a strong foundation, so should you never enter a conversation without a focus on creating a psychologically safe space. The tools we've explored—ground rules, non-verbal cues, the pause and reflect technique, and understanding conflict resolution styles—are your building blocks.

As you move forward, remember that the art of conversation is a skill, not a talent. Skills get better with practice. So don't hesitate to apply what you've learned here in your day-to-day interactions.

And so, as we close this chapter, ask yourself: How will you lay the first brick in constructing your next safe conversational space? The next leg of our journey will introduce even more tools and strategies, so keep your architect's hat on; we're just getting started.

Ready to take a breather and reflect? We'll dive into that in our next pit stop for reflection.

Pit Stop for Reflection: Creating a Safe Space

Before we forge ahead, let's take a moment to pause and reflect. Think of this as your 'rest area' on this journey through the dynamics of conflict and conversation.

1. Recalling Safe Spaces: Can you recall a situation where you felt psychologically safe during a difficult conversation? How did that impact the dialogue?
2. Actionable Steps: What are some actionable steps you can take to create a safe space in your next challenging conversation? Consider the ground rules and techniques we've discussed.
3. Vulnerability Check: When was the last time you showed vulnerability in a conversation? What was the outcome? Did it align with the 'Vulnerability Paradox' we explored?
4. Trust and Safety: Do you find it easier to trust someone in a conversation when you feel safe? Why or why not?
5. The Ripple Effect: Have you experienced the ripple effect of one good, open conversation changing the dynamics of a relationship or team setting? Share that experience.

Take your time with these questions. Write down your thoughts if you can. Remember, the aim is not to rush through but to deepen your understanding and personalize these concepts.

Now, as you finish this pit stop, gear up. The road ahead has more to offer, and you're better equipped than ever to navigate it.

Chapter 6: The Socratic Method

"The unexamined life is not worth living."

— Socrates

I magine walking through the bustling marketplace of ancient Athens, where philosophers and thinkers of antiquity gathered to share their insights. Amidst the clamor, you find Socrates, an unassuming figure who would go on to change the landscape of critical thinking. Rather than preaching or lecturing, Socrates had a different approach: he asked questions. Not just any questions, but those designed to spark introspection, challenge assumptions, and provoke a deeper understanding of life's complexities.

Fast forward to today. You're not in Athens, and the marketplace is perhaps a heated family dinner, a tense boardroom, or a dispute with a friend. The setting may have changed, but the need for meaningful dialogue is just as pressing. And that's where the Socratic Method comes in. A tool rooted in the past but immensely relevant for today, it serves as a bridge between opposing viewpoints, a way to illuminate hidden biases, and a means to arrive at truth—or at least, a better understanding of it.

In this chapter, we will unearth the principles of the Socratic Method and decode its enduring legacy. More importantly, we'll translate this time-honored technique into practical steps you can take to enhance your own conversations and conflicts. From the agora of Athens to the living rooms, workplaces, and social spaces of today, we will explore how the Socratic Method can be a transformative tool for dialogue.

Ready to explore this rich terrain? Let's begin.

Origins and Philosophy

The Socratic Method finds its origins in the intellectual climate of ancient Athens, specifically in the teachings of Socrates, a philosopher who lived from 469 to 399 BCE. Unlike his contemporaries, who often espoused grand theories about the nature of the universe, Socrates took a decidedly different route. He was less concerned with declaring what he knew and more interested in questioning what others thought they knew. He believed that through questioning, people could arrive at a clearer, more nuanced understanding of complex issues, from ethics to politics to the human condition itself.

The Socratic Method is essentially a form of cooperative argumentative dialogue. But let's break that down. "Cooperative" signifies that the method is not about winning an argument but about working together to reach a deeper understanding. "Argumentative" doesn't mean quarrelsome here; rather, it refers to the structured, logical form of the dialogue. The focus is on "dialogue," a two-way interaction, instead of a monologue where one person does all the talking.

The core philosophy behind this method is rooted in the principle of "elenchus," a Greek term that means examination or refutation. The aim isn't to challenge for the sake of causing discord, but rather to stimulate critical thinking. By asking questions that challenge assumptions and provoke introspection, Socrates guided people toward illuminating previously unexplored ideas. In a way, it's like turning on a flashlight in a dark room. Suddenly, objects that were always there but unseen become visible. Similarly, the Socratic Method brings to light assumptions, beliefs, and thought patterns that often go unnoticed but significantly influence our attitudes and behaviors.

The beauty of this method lies in its simplicity. It doesn't require advanced degrees or specialized knowledge. All it requires is curiosity—a desire to understand not just what someone is saying, but why they're saying it. And this is why the method has endured through the ages, from the marble steps of ancient academies to the modern classrooms, courtrooms, and even counseling sessions. It's a timeless tool for fostering critical thinking and illuminating the caverns of our understanding.

In essence, the Socratic Method is not just a debating technique or a scholarly strategy. It's a lens through which we can view dialogue, a framework that elevates conversation from mere transaction to meaningful interaction.

So, how can a method formulated over two millennia ago in the heart of ancient Greece be relevant to your next heated argument or complex decision? Stick with me, and you'll find out.

Historical Context

The Socratic Method didn't emerge in a vacuum. To fully grasp its significance, it's essential to place it within the broader context of ancient Greek society, a civilization that placed a high value on public discourse and the pursuit of knowledge.

In ancient Athens, the public square, or "Agora," was more than just a marketplace; it was the hub of intellectual and political life. Philosophers, statesmen, and ordinary citizens would gather to discuss issues of public concern, from the governance of the city-state to the nature of virtue and justice. Here, Socrates became a familiar figure, engaging people from all walks of life in his unique form of dialogue. Unlike the Sophists of his time, who charged hefty fees for their teachings, Socrates believed that wisdom should be freely shared and collectively pursued. His method was a democratic one, open to anyone willing to engage in honest, thoughtful conversation.

The impact of the Socratic Method wasn't confined to Athens or even to ancient Greece. It left an indelible mark on Western thought and became a cornerstone of the educational system. Over the centuries, this method has been adopted and adapted by countless thinkers, from medieval scholars to Enlightenment philosophers to contemporary educators. It became an essential tool for fostering the kind of critical thinking that is the bedrock of a democratic society. Even today, the Socratic Method is used in various settings, from law schools where students are trained to think like a lawyer, to corporate boardrooms where complex problems require nuanced solutions.

Moreover, the method has transcended cultural and historical boundaries, finding relevance in diverse contexts and disciplines. Whether it's ethical debates in medical schools or strategic discussions in business meetings, the core principles of inquiry, dialogue, and critical thinking remain universally applicable.

So, why has this method endured over the millennia, and how can it be applied in today's complex, fast-paced world? The answer lies in its fundamental utility. The Socratic Method isn't just a historical artifact; it's a living, breathing approach to dialogue that adapts to the needs and challenges of any era, including our own.

The historical richness and enduring legacy of the Socratic Method serve as a testament to its effectiveness. But more than that, they invite us to consider how this ancient approach to dialogue can be a vital tool for resolving the conflicts and misunderstandings that are all too common in our modern lives.

Enduring Legacy

Now, you might be wondering, why has a method developed over two millennia ago not only survived but thrived? The Socratic Method has an enduring legacy precisely because it addresses a universal human need: the quest for understanding. This is not limited to any one period or culture; it's a constant across human history.

The method's influence has been far-reaching. In academia, it forms the backbone of the "Socratic seminar," a teaching strategy that encourages students to discuss complex topics openly and critically. In the legal world, "Socratic questioning" is a staple in classrooms and courtrooms alike, designed to probe the underlying assumptions and principles that govern the law. Even in the realms of psychology and counseling, the Socratic Method finds its echoes. For example, cognitive-behavioral therapy often employs Socratic questioning to challenge irrational beliefs and cognitive distortions.

But its legacy goes beyond formal settings. The Socratic Method permeates our everyday interactions as well. When you engage in a deep discussion with a friend, probing the reasons behind your beliefs, or when you question the assumptions underlying a heated family debate, you're employing principles that Socrates would have endorsed. The method teaches us to value the journey of questioning as much as, if not more than, the destination of knowing.

What gives the Socratic Method its lasting relevance is its adaptability. It serves as a scaffold, a structure upon which any dialogue can be built, regardless of the subject matter or the participants involved. This method doesn't provide answers; instead, it offers a way to seek them, encouraging open dialogue and critical thinking. It turns the act of conversation into a cooperative endeavor, where the goal is not to win an argument, but to gain a deeper understanding of the issue—and of each other.

So, can this ancient tool really be applied to modern conflicts, from boardrooms to living rooms?

Its Application in Modern-Day Conflicts

The Socratic Method is not confined to the hallowed halls of academia or the depths of philosophical debate. Its principles are universally applicable, and its methods can be employed in the most everyday of situations. Imagine transitioning this method from the Agora—the ancient Greek marketplace where Socrates often engaged in dialogue—to your own living room. How would that look?

The key to the Socratic Method is its focus on questions rather than answers. Picture this: you're in the middle of a heated argument with your partner. Rather than tossing accusations or defending your viewpoint, you pause and ask a question, "Can you help me understand what you're feeling right now?" This simple act of asking not only gives your partner space to express themselves but also encourages you to genuinely listen.

The beauty of applying the Socratic Method in personal relationships or professional settings lies in its ability to unearth the underlying issues that often fuel conflicts. It becomes less about who is right and more about understanding the foundational beliefs and emotions driving the disagreement. This shift in focus from 'winning' the argument to understanding the core issues can be transformative.

Moreover, the method encourages self-reflection. When you ask open-ended, probing questions, you're not only inviting the other person to think deeply but also reflecting on your own beliefs and assumptions. This two-way street of mutual exploration creates a dynamic where both parties are invested in understanding, rather than defeating, each other.

Questioning as a Tool

We've established that the Socratic Method is all about asking questions. But not just any questions—purposeful, probing ones designed to peel back the layers of an argument, assumption, or belief. Have you ever been in a conversation where the other person made a sweeping statement that you didn't quite agree with? Your gut reaction might be to counter with your own statement. But what if, instead, you asked a question?

Let's say your colleague claims, "Our project is doomed to fail because we don't have enough resources." Instead of immediately disagreeing or defending your viewpoint, you could ask, "What specific resources do you think we're lacking?" This question not only opens up room for clarification but also challenges the initial sweeping statement. It's a pivot from a potentially confrontational stance to one of inquiry and understanding.

Questions serve multiple functions in a conversation, especially one that's heated or divisive. First, they force a pause in the conversation, a brief moment where both parties can step back from their emotional precipice. Second, they encourage reflection. When you ask a question, you're inviting the other person to think more deeply about their stance. What are the assumptions underlying their viewpoint? Are those assumptions valid? And third, questions can dismantle prejudices or diffuse tension. They cut through the noise of our preconceived notions and bring us back to the fundamental issues at hand.

The power of questioning in the Socratic Method lies in its ability to turn the conversation from a battlefield into an exploration terrain. Instead of weapons, you have tools—questions aimed at carving out a shared understanding from a mountain of differing opinions.

The Role of Humility

In a world that often equates confidence with competence, humility might seem like an unlikely hero in conflict resolution. But make no mistake, adopting a Socratic stance involves a deep recognition that you don't have all the answers. And that's more powerful than it sounds. Have you ever encountered someone who seemed to know it all? How willing were you to open up to that person, to share your own insights or admit your uncertainties?

When you approach a conversation with humility, you're sending out a signal—a subtle but impactful invitation for the other party to step into the dialogue as an equal. No one likes to be lectured. Most of us can sense when we're being talked at rather than talked with. A humble approach shifts the dynamic. It says, "I value your perspective. Teach me what you know, so we can learn together."

Humility isn't about diminishing yourself or your knowledge; it's about creating room for others. It's the act of making space in the conversation for multiple truths and multiple experiences. This is especially vital in conflicts where emotions run high, and stakes are even higher. By consciously choosing humility, you're laying down your conversational arms, so to speak, and picking up tools of construction instead. You transition from building walls to building bridges.

Think about this for a moment. How often do you enter a difficult conversation already convinced of your own rightness? What if, the next time you find yourself in such a situation, you took a deep breath and reminded yourself that you don't have all the answers? How might that simple shift in mindset change the trajectory of the conversation?

Humility in the Socratic Method is far from a sign of weakness; it's a hallmark of conversational maturity. And in a conflict, it might just be the key that unlocks a more meaningful, constructive dialogue.

Practical Examples and Exercises

If knowledge is the map, then application is the journey. We've journeyed through the philosophical and historical underpinnings of the Socratic Method, and now it's time to put those principles to work in the real world. This section is the hands-on lab to the theoretical lecture, a space where you can roll up your sleeves and get your conversational hands dirty. We'll walk through specific types of Socratic questions you can employ, see a real-world dialogue in action, and even craft your own 'question bank' for future use. Ready to move from theory to practice?

The Socratic Question Types

The Socratic Method is not a one-size-fits-all approach; it's a toolkit, filled with different types of questions designed to prod, probe, and illuminate. Understanding these question types can turn you into a conversational craftsman, skillfully choosing the right tool for the moment.

- Clarifying Questions: These are your bread and butter when you're confused or when you suspect that maybe the other person hasn't fully unpacked their thoughts. Questions like, "Can you elaborate on that?" or "What do you mean when you say X?" can make the fuzzy contours of an idea much sharper.

- Probing Assumptions: Assumptions are the hidden drivers behind most conflicts. Probing them is like checking the foundation of a house before you decide to move in. "What are you assuming that leads you to that conclusion?" or "How did you arrive at that idea?" can unearth hidden presuppositions.

- Questioning Viewpoints and Perspectives: Sometimes people get locked into a particular viewpoint and struggle to see outside it. Questions like, "Have you considered the opposite perspective?" or "What would someone who disagrees with you say?" can broaden the horizon of a conversation.

- Probing Implications and Consequences: These questions examine the downstream effects of a particular stance or decision. "What would happen if we followed your suggestion?" or "How does this align with our overall goals?" can help both parties think beyond the immediate moment.

- Questions About the Question: Sometimes, the issue is with the framing of the question itself. "Why do you think this question is important?" or "What does answering this question help us achieve?" can reveal the underlying issues that really need addressing.

Consider these types as options in your conversational toolkit. The next time you find yourself in a heated debate or a tough conversation, try implementing these question types. Notice how the conversation shifts, how the ground becomes a bit more stable, and the air a bit clearer.

Socratic Dialogue in Action

It's one thing to understand the Socratic Method in theory, but watching it unfold in a live conversation is an entirely different experience. Imagine you're a fly on the wall during a heated family dinner. Aunt Emily believes that all young people are lazy and entitled, while you disagree but want to approach the subject tactfully. How could the Socratic Method be employed here?

- Clarifying Questions: "Aunt Emily, could you help me understand what you mean when you say all young people are lazy?"

- Probing Assumptions: "What experiences or examples led you to that conclusion?"

- Questioning Viewpoints: "Have you considered that economic conditions have changed since you were their age?"

- Exploring Implications: "What do you think would change if society as a whole adopted your viewpoint?"
- Questioning the Original Question: "Is the behavior of an entire generation a fair measure for determining their worth or capabilities?"

In this example, not only do the questions aim to clarify Aunt Emily's position, but they also provoke critical thinking and potentially pave the way for a more nuanced understanding of the issue at hand. Now, Aunt Emily may not suddenly recant her views, but the questions could plant seeds of doubt or, at the very least, offer her a new perspective to consider.

The "Question Bank" Exercise

It's said that knowledge is power, but in the realm of conflict resolution, the right question at the right time can be equally powerful. This exercise is designed to help you build your own 'Question Bank' of Socratic questions that can serve as your arsenal in various conflict scenarios you commonly encounter.

1. Identify Scenarios: First, think of three conflict scenarios you often find yourself in. These could be workplace disputes, familial disagreements, or social tensions.
2. Draft Questions: For each scenario, draft at least five Socratic questions aimed at delving deeper into the issue. These could range from clarifying questions like "Can you help me understand your point of view?" to probing assumptions such as "What leads you to believe that?"
3. Review and Refine: After creating the list, review each question. Is it likely to elicit a thoughtful response? If not, refine it.
4. Practice: The next time you find yourself in one of these scenarios, refer to your Question Bank and select one or two questions to use. Take note of how the conversation shifts as a result.
5. Reflect and Update: After the conflict, take some time to reflect. Did the questions open up the dialogue? Did they help you and the other party reach a deeper understanding? Update your Question Bank accordingly.

This exercise not only makes you more prepared for conflicts but also equips you with the tools to navigate them more constructively. Think of your Question Bank as a living document, something you can continually update and refine as you gain more experience.

Do you find the idea of a "Question Bank" helpful for your personal growth? Would you consider implementing it in your daily life?

Wrapping Up Chapter 6: The Socratic Method

As we close this chapter, let's take a moment to appreciate the profound wisdom embedded in the Socratic Method—a philosophical tool as ancient as it is enduring. Whether you're in the workplace, at home, or anywhere in between, the art of asking the right questions can unlock doors to deeper understanding and meaningful resolution.

We've explored the historical roots of this method, discussed its modern-day applications, and even looked into some hands-on exercises to help you put this age-old wisdom into practice. Your Question Bank, if cultivated diligently, can become a go-to resource for navigating tricky conversations, effectively transforming conflicts into opportunities for growth and connection.

The Socratic Method serves as a timeless reminder that questions, when asked with genuine curiosity and openness, can be far more powerful than assertions. So, the next time you find yourself in a conflict, remember Socrates and his love for good questions. It might just lead you down a path of discovery and reconciliation you never thought possible.

Are you ready to make Socratic questioning a part of your conflict resolution toolkit? If you are, the vistas of understanding it can open are truly limitless.

In the next chapter, we'll continue building on these skills, adding more layers to your ever-growing understanding of conflict transformation.

Pit Stop for Reflection: Self Contemplation

As we pause at the end of this enriching chapter, it's time for some contemplation and self-assessment.

- Questioning as a Tool: Have you ever used questioning as a tool for understanding in a conflict? What was the outcome? Reflect on the situation, and consider how using Socratic questioning might have altered the course of that dialogue.

- Your Question Bank: What are some questions you could add to your own 'question bank' for future conflicts? Think about common situations where you find yourself at odds with someone. What questions could you ask to clarify their viewpoint or to examine the assumptions underlying the disagreement?

Take a few minutes to ponder these questions and jot down your thoughts. This is an essential step toward internalizing the concepts we've discussed and making them practical tools in your conversational arsenal.

Your understanding and application of the Socratic Method could be the game-changer in your next conflict situation. So, are you ready to take Socratic dialogue off the ancient Greek stage and bring it into your living room?

Interlude: Toolkit for Constructive Conversations

Welcome to this interlude, the toolkit for constructive conversations. Think of it as your conversational "first aid kit"—the go-to guide you can reach for when the stakes are high and emotions are running hot. We've been on quite a journey so far, covering the terrain of emotional triggers, empathy, active listening, and the art of asking questions. Now, it's time to consolidate all these insights into a practical guide.

So why have we strategically placed this toolkit here, at the end of Part II? Simply put, it's designed to serve as a quick reference guide that distills the essence of what you've learned so far into actionable steps. It's like having a cheat sheet during an exam; except here, the 'exam' is any challenging conversation you might find yourself in. Whether you're grappling with a heated argument with a loved one or navigating a complex negotiation at work, this toolkit is designed to be your lifeline.

You can interact with this toolkit in two main ways: as a study guide or as an emergency reference. If you're using it as a study guide, take your time to dive into each section, practicing the exercises and reflecting on how they relate to your own experiences. On the other hand, if you're in the heat of a difficult conversation, feel free to skim through to the tool or technique that seems most applicable for the situation at hand.

Compilation of Tools and Techniques

Alright, let's roll up our sleeves and dive into the core of this toolkit. Here, we're going to compile the most effective tools and techniques we've discussed in the previous chapters. Consider this section your "Swiss Army knife" for handling conflicts and fostering constructive conversations.

Active Listening Techniques

Remember Chapter 4, where we dissected the art of active listening? Well, it's time for a quick refresher. Active listening is not just about hearing the words; it's about understanding the message behind them. Here's a quick "how-to" and "when-to-use" guide:

- Paraphrasing: After the other person has spoken, rephrase what they've said in your own words. This ensures that you've understood them correctly and signals that you are engaged. Use this when the conversation is complex or emotionally charged.
- Open-Ended Questions: These are questions that can't be answered with a simple 'yes' or 'no.' They invite the speaker to share more, which can be particularly useful in uncovering underlying issues. Use these when you feel the conversation is superficial and needs to go deeper.
- Nodding and Eye Contact: Simple, yet effective. These non-verbal cues say, "I'm with you; keep going." Use these consistently but naturally throughout the conversation.

Creating a Safe Space

Ah, the sanctity of a safe space. Recall Chapter 5, where we explored the concept of psychological safety in conversations. Here's a snapshot of actionable steps for you:

- Ground Rules: Before diving into a difficult topic, consider establishing some basic rules like no interruptions or confirming understanding before moving on. This sets the tone for a respectful and constructive dialogue.
- Non-Verbal Cues: Remember, your body talks even when you're silent. Maintain eye contact, use open postures, and nod occasionally to build an atmosphere of trust and openness.
- Affirmations: Briefly acknowledge the other person's points or feelings, even if you don't agree. Phrases like "I see where you're coming from" can go a long way.

The Socratic Question Bank

A nod to Chapter 6, where we looked into the age-old wisdom of the Socratic Method. Here's your own question bank, tailored for conflict scenarios:

- Clarifying Questions: "Can you help me understand what you meant by that?"
- Probing Assumptions: "What leads you to believe that this is the best course of action?"
- Questioning Viewpoints: "Have you considered the implications of this on other team members?"

Use these questions when you feel that the conversation is becoming confrontational, or when you sense that underlying assumptions need to be unearthed.

Would you agree that having these techniques at your fingertips could make navigating tricky conversations a bit easier?

Emotional Self-Check

The emotional landscape is treacherous if left unexplored. Remember our discussions on emotional triggers and empathy in Part I? Here's a quick refresher:

- Trigger Journal: Keep this handy. Note instances where you felt emotionally charged, and later analyze them to understand your emotional patterns.
- Empathy Gauge: Before entering a tough conversation, rate your empathy level on a scale of 1-10. Aim to increase it by at least one point during the discussion.

Quick Exercises for Real-Time Application

Sometimes, you need a quick fix. A small adjustment can bring a conversation back from the brink of disaster. Here are some rapid-response tools:

- The "Three Breath Pause": Feel your emotions rising? Take three deep breaths. This simple act can reset your emotional state, allowing you to approach the situation with newfound clarity.

- The Clarifying Statement: Uncertainty breeds conflict. If you're unsure, use a clarifying statement like, "Let me make sure I understand what you're saying..." This opens the door for the other person to provide more context.
- The Empathy Prompt: To shift focus back to emotional understanding, employ a question like, "How did that make you feel?" This can defuse tension and pave the way for a more empathic dialogue.

Troubleshooting: Navigating the Roadblocks

In the journey toward constructive conversations, even the most well-intentioned traveler may hit some bumps along the way. You've been armed with a toolkit, but what happens when the tools don't seem to work as expected? This section is your guide for those less-than-smooth moments, offering you solutions for common challenges you may encounter.

When Active Listening Doesn't Seem to Work

You're nodding, paraphrasing, and asking open-ended questions, but the other person seems disengaged or even hostile. What now?

- Check Your Timing: Sometimes the problem isn't the tool, but when it's being used. Are you trying to listen actively to someone who is in the middle of a crisis or an emotional outburst? It might not be the right time for nuanced communication skills.
- Reflect on Your Non-Verbal Cues: Are your facial expressions and body language in sync with your verbal active listening cues? A furrowed brow or crossed arms could be sending mixed messages.
- Clarify Intent: It might be helpful to explicitly state that you're trying to understand their point of view. Sometimes stating your positive intent can break down walls.

Overcoming Resistance to the Socratic Method

The Socratic Method can be powerful, but not everyone takes kindly to being questioned. How can you make this age-old technique feel like a conversation rather than an interrogation?

- Set the Stage: Before diving into Socratic questioning, explain that you're asking questions to better understand, not to challenge or confront.
- Be Mindful of Tone and Pacing: A rapid-fire sequence of questions can feel overwhelming. Keep your tone gentle and allow space for the other person to think and respond.
- Know When to Switch Gears: If you sense resistance, it might be wise to switch to a more straightforward form of communication. Sometimes a direct statement is more effective than a question.

Navigating Emotional Minefields

Difficult conversations often veer into emotionally charged territory. How can you steer them back to a more neutral ground?

- Recognize Emotional Triggers: Your toolkit includes the knowledge of emotional triggers. Use this awareness to detect when the conversation is hitting a raw nerve, either for you or the other person.
- Use the 'Three Breath Pause': When emotions run high, it's easy to react rather than respond. Recalling the "Three Breath Pause" exercise from your toolkit can create a much-needed moment of clarity.
- Engage Empathy: When in doubt, empathy is often the best tool for navigating emotional terrain. Try using the "Empathy Prompt" from your toolkit to refocus the conversation on feelings rather than contentious issues.

PART THREE
Advanced Techniques & Application

Chapter 7: The Alchemy of Apology

*"An apology is the superglue of life. It can repair just
about anything."*

– Lynn Johnston

In a world where misunderstandings and disagreements are as
commonplace as the air we breathe, there exists an elixir with the power
to mend fractured relationships and heal emotional wounds. This
transformative potion isn't sold in mystical shops, nor is it the stuff of fairy
tales. It's the art of the genuine apology, a simple yet profound set of words
and actions that can change the course of human interactions.

If you've ever found yourself wrestling with the weight of a conflict,
you know how a single sentence like "I'm sorry" can either dissipate the
tension or escalate it, depending on its sincerity. But what if I told you that
the true art of apologizing goes far beyond those two words? What if I told
you that mastering this art could not only resolve conflicts but also deepen
your relationships and catalyze personal growth?

Welcome to "The Alchemy of Apology," where we'll investigate the
psychology and power of a genuine apology, provide a step-by-step guide to
make your apologies impactful, and explore the liberating role of forgiveness.
Hold tight, because you're about to learn a skill that can turn even the most
fraught conflicts into opportunities for profound emotional connection and
growth. Shall we begin?

What Makes an Apology

At first glance, an apology seems straightforward enough—a simple
"I'm sorry" should suffice, right? But if you've ever been on the receiving end
of a half-hearted apology, you'll know that those two words can sometimes

feel as hollow as a drum. So, what distinguishes a genuine apology from an insincere one? Let's break it down into its core elements:

#1: Acknowledgment of Wrongdoing: The first step in a meaningful apology is acknowledging the wrong that has been done. This involves clearly stating what the offense was without using any "ifs" or "buts" to dilute the acknowledgment. This is not the time for vague phrases like "If I hurt you" or "I'm sorry you feel that way." Rather, it's about being explicit: "I was wrong to raise my voice at you," or "I shouldn't have ignored your calls."

#2: Display of Empathy: The next layer involves showing genuine empathy for the person you've wronged. Empathy is the emotional glue that connects people; it's about putting yourself in the other person's shoes and feeling their pain as if it were your own. In the context of an apology, this means conveying that you understand the emotional impact of your actions: "I can imagine that what I did made you feel disrespected and hurt."

#3: Commitment to Make Amends :A genuine apology comes with the promise of future change, a commitment to make amends. Saying sorry without any intention to avoid repeating the offending action is like putting a band-aid on a wound without cleaning it first—it's unlikely to foster true healing. Therefore, part of your apology should involve outlining the steps you intend to take to avoid repeating the mistake: "I will make an effort to be more attentive to your needs moving forward."

By incorporating these three elements, you transform a superficial "I'm sorry" into a profound, meaningful apology that has the power to heal and transform relationships. Think of it like a carefully crafted recipe: each ingredient is essential, and when combined in the right proportions, they create something far greater than the sum of its parts.

The Psychological Impact of a Genuine Apology

Imagine you're carrying a backpack filled with stones, each stone representing a grievance or a hurt. With each careless word or deed from someone else, the weight becomes heavier. You could, of course, continue to trudge along, your back stooped and your steps sluggish, but what a relief it would be if even one of those stones were lifted! That's precisely what a genuine apology can do—it has the power to remove a stone, lighten the load, and change the trajectory of an emotional journey. Let's explore how.

Receiving a genuine apology serves as a form of emotional validation. When someone acknowledges their wrongdoing, it confirms that your feelings are legitimate. You are no longer a ship lost in the stormy seas of doubt and invalidation; you have found your harbor. This validation is an important steppingstone for emotional healing. It acts as confirmation that what you felt was real, and that alone can be incredibly liberating. Have you ever felt the weight lifted off your shoulders when someone genuinely acknowledged their mistake?

An apology, when done right, can act as a catalyst for emotional healing. In the chemical world, a catalyst is a substance that speeds up a reaction without itself undergoing any change. Similarly, a genuine apology can accelerate the process of moving from hurt to forgiveness, from conflict to resolution. It creates a space where both parties can breathe, reassess, and begin to rebuild. It also provides a sense of closure, a demarcation point that both parties can refer back to as the moment when the healing began. Have you experienced such a transformative moment?

An apology doesn't just mend emotional fences; it can also serve as a bridge between opposing viewpoints. Once an apology is offered and accepted, it sets the stage for constructive dialogue. The atmosphere changes: defensive walls come down, and the focus shifts from blame to mutual understanding. The apology acts as a reset button, allowing for a more meaningful and less emotionally charged exchange. This is where problem-solving can genuinely occur.

In a nutshell, the psychological impact of a genuine apology is multi-layered and profound. It validates, it heals, and it paves the way for constructive conflict resolution. It's like emotional alchemy, transforming the base metal of hurt and misunderstanding into the gold of connection and mutual respect.

The Healing Ingredient

An apology can be likened to a medicinal herb in the garden of human interactions—an herb that has the potential to heal wounds and mend relationships. But what exactly is the healing ingredient in an apology that makes it so potent? Is it the act of acknowledging wrongdoing, or is there more to it?

The first layer of the healing ingredient in an apology is the acknowledgment of the other person's pain or discomfort. This acknowledgment acts as a salve on the wound. It's the first step in the healing process, serving to clean the injury and prepare it for further treatment. Could you think of a time when someone acknowledging their mistake changed the emotional temperature of the room?

The next layer involves empathy, a powerful emotional tool. When someone apologizes and shows genuine understanding of how their actions have affected you, it's akin to applying an antibiotic ointment to the wound. This not only speeds up the healing process but also creates an emotional environment less prone to future infections of resentment and anger. Have you ever noticed how much easier it is to forgive someone when you feel they genuinely understand your perspective?

Finally, a meaningful apology always involves a commitment to make amends. This is the final touch, the bandage that protects the wound as it heals. The commitment to make amends shows that the person is not just sorry for the past but is also willing to work towards a better future. It's a forward-looking aspect of the apology that offers hope and reassurance.

So, the healing ingredient of a genuine apology is not just one thing; it's a blend of acknowledgment, empathy, and a commitment to make amends. It's a carefully balanced formula that, when applied correctly, has the power to heal emotional wounds and set the stage for a renewed relationship. It turns the act of apologizing into a form of emotional alchemy, a magical transformation that can lead to deeper connections and a more harmonious existence.

Steps to Make an Impactful Apology

An apology is like a key that can unlock doors that seemed forever closed, but not all keys fit all locks. An apology needs to be crafted with precision, much like a master key, to open the door to reconciliation and understanding. So how do you go about crafting such a key?

The Four Rs

In the realm of meaningful apologies, let's consider a framework known as the Four Rs: Recognition, Responsibility, Remorse, and Repair.

Recognition: The first step is recognizing that you've done something wrong. Without this acknowledgment, an apology lacks its foundational stone. Recognizing a mistake is akin to a musician tuning their instrument before a performance. Ever notice how different a situation feels when someone genuinely acknowledges what they've done?

Responsibility: Taking responsibility for your actions adds weight to your words. It moves the apology from a passive statement to an active acknowledgment of your role in the situation. This is the structure upon which the rest of the apology is built. Have you ever felt more inclined to forgive someone who not only recognized their mistake but also took responsibility for it?

Remorse: Expressing genuine remorse is where the emotional labor of apologizing truly lies. Remorse shows that you don't just understand the intellectual aspects of your mistake, but you also feel the emotional weight of your actions. It's the soul of the apology. Can you recall a time when someone's expressed remorse touched you deeply?

Repair: The final R stands for Repair, which is the commitment to make amends and ensure the mistake doesn't happen again. It's the promise of a new melody in the ongoing composition of your relationship. It gives the person you're apologizing to a reason to trust you again. What does a commitment to making amends look like to you? Could you identify this in any past experiences?

The Timing and Setting

Imagine an artist choosing the right moment to reveal a masterpiece. Timing and setting can make a significant difference, not just in art but also in the impact of an apology. Let's dig into why that is.

Timing: An ill-timed apology can feel rushed or insincere, like reading the last page of a novel first. It's crucial to find a moment when both you and the other person have the emotional and mental space to engage in the conversation. Ever been in a situation where someone apologized at the wrong time, and it felt like they were just trying to "get it over with"?

Setting: The environment in which you apologize also matters immensely. A noisy, crowded place may not be the best setting for heartfelt words. It's like trying to listen to a delicate symphony in the middle of a bustling market. The message may get lost. A private, quiet space where the conversation can flow without external interruptions often works best. Can you think of an instance where the setting profoundly affected the impact of an apology?

In essence, timing and setting are the stage and backdrop for your apology, and choosing them wisely can mean the difference between a standing ovation and a lukewarm response.

Words vs. Actions

We've all heard the saying, "Actions speak louder than words," haven't we? But what does this mean in the context of an apology?

The Role of Words: Words are the starting point, the initial step in mending a broken bridge. They articulate regret, acknowledge harm, and promise better behavior. However, words alone can sometimes feel like a hollow promise, a contract with no intent behind it. How many times have you heard "I'm sorry," only to see the same mistake repeated?

The Power of Actions: This is where actions come into play. They are the follow-through, the execution of the contract made by your words. Think of it as planting a seed with your apology and then nurturing it with your actions. If you say you're sorry and promise not to repeat the mistake, your actions must demonstrate this commitment. It's the equivalent of showing up to the gym after declaring, "I will get in shape."

The Symbiosis: Words and actions, in the context of an apology, are like a melody and its lyrics; one complements the other. Saying sorry opens the door, but it's your subsequent actions that invite someone to walk through it. A well-timed "I'm sorry" followed by meaningful actions can turn a moment of conflict into an opportunity for growth and deepened connection.

Would you agree that an apology feels incomplete without the weight of actions to give it substance?

The Role of Forgiveness

If we were to envision the process of apologizing and forgiving as an intricate work of art, forgiveness would be the final brushstroke that completes the painting. It's the moment when the artist steps back, brushes in hand, and recognizes that the canvas is complete, that the emotional landscape has shifted, and transformation has occurred. This is not just any brushstroke; it's the one that brings balance, unity, and resolution to the chaotic mix of colors and emotions that preceded it. It's the stroke that says, "This chapter is closed, and a new one can now begin."

In musical terms, forgiveness is the resolving note in a complex composition, the chord that brings a sense of completion and peace after a series of dissonant and turbulent passages. Just as that final note can make a listener's heart swell with emotion, the act of forgiveness floods our emotional landscape with a sense of relief and resolution. It's the moment where tension gives way to tranquility, where discord transforms into harmony.

So why is this final act so potent? Why does it feel like alchemy? Because in that one brushstroke or resolving note—i.e., the act of forgiveness—the base metals of hurt and misunderstanding are transmuted into the gold of emotional freedom and deeper connection. It's where the alchemy of apology reaches its zenith. And much like an alchemist, you're not just changing the substance in front of you; you're also transforming something deep within yourself.

Forgiveness as Liberation

In the realm of emotional dynamics, forgiveness is often misconceived as merely a selfless act—one that serves the person being forgiven more than the forgiver. This perspective, while understandable, falls short of capturing the full spectrum of what forgiveness can accomplish.

Imagine carrying around a heavy backpack filled with stones, each one representing an unresolved conflict or a grudge. This backpack burdens your steps, hunches your back, and drains your energy. You carry it everywhere, and it weighs on you in every interaction, every decision, and even invades your dreams. The backpack becomes a part of you—a part that constrains your freedom and dims your joy.

Now, let's consider the act of forgiveness as an intentional process of reaching into that backpack and removing those stones one by one. Each stone removed lightens your load, straightens your posture, and frees up emotional energy that you can direct toward more constructive pursuits. You're no longer pulled back by the weight of past conflicts; you're propelled forward by the liberation of present forgiveness.

100

Isn't it fascinating that an act aimed at granting someone else peace—freeing them from their own backpack of stones, so to speak—can bring you so much tranquility and freedom? It's like an emotional boomerang: what you give comes back to you, sometimes in ways you didn't expect. By granting forgiveness, you're not just unburdening another person; you're unburdening yourself.

Have you ever experienced the weight of such a "backpack"? Have you ever felt the liberation that comes from taking those stones out? If so, did it change your view on what forgiveness truly means?

The Two-Part Equation: The Humbling Dance of Apology and Acceptance

Apologizing and forgiving can often feel like a dance—a choreographed sequence where both partners must be in sync for the dance to be truly harmonious. However, it's important to remember that this dance is a two-part equation, and it's not always balanced. You can execute your steps with grace and sincerity, but the other person has to be willing to dance with you for the sequence to reach its full potential.

When you apologize, you're essentially initiating the dance. You step onto the emotional dance floor with a sincere "I'm sorry," your eyes meeting theirs, your intent laid bare. You've done your part; you've extended your hand, inviting them into this dance of reconciliation. But here's the humbling truth: They can either accept your invitation and step forward or decline and step back. Either way, the next move is theirs to make.

This realization can be both liberating and humbling. Liberating because once you've made your sincere apology, you've done your part. The weight of the wrongdoing is lifted from your shoulders the moment your apology leaves your lips. Humbling because you come face to face with the reality that you can't control someone else's emotional journey. You can't force them to forgive; you can only create the conditions that make forgiveness more likely.

The "Forgiveness Letter" Exercise: Putting Pen to Paper for Emotional Healing

In a world where texts and tweets have often replaced long-form communication, there's something incredibly raw and potent about putting pen to paper. It's almost as if the act of writing captures the essence of your emotional state, crystallizing it into a form that can be touched and held. But why is this exercise so transformative, especially when dealing with the nuanced emotions around forgiveness?

Imagine you're an alchemist, and your words are the ingredients for a potent elixir—the Elixir of Emotional Healing, if you will. Each sentence you write either asking for or granting forgiveness serves as a crucial component in this healing brew.

For Those Seeking Forgiveness

If you are the one seeking forgiveness, your letter is your opportunity to distill your remorse, your understanding of the hurt caused, and your commitment to change into a potent, heartfelt message. In it, you can express the nuances of your regret that spoken words might not fully capture. You articulate your wrongdoings clearly, without excuses, showing that you recognize the pain you've caused. You express your feelings of sorrow and pen your commitment to change, offering a vision of a future where such hurt won't be repeated.

For Those Granting Forgiveness

On the flip side, if you are the one granting forgiveness, your letter becomes a symbolic act of releasing the emotional baggage you've been carrying. The words you write aren't just ink on paper; they are the symbolic stones you remove from your heavy backpack of resentment and hurt. With each sentence, you lighten your emotional load, giving yourself the gift of freedom from the past.

The Therapeutic Power of Writing

In both scenarios, the act of writing serves dual purposes. First, it forces you to confront your emotions, to name them, and in doing so, to tame them. Second, it provides a tangible artifact—a piece of emotional history—that you can hold in your hands, read and re-read, and even share if the situation warrants it. It makes the abstract concrete, the unspoken spoken, and the internal external.

So, would you consider writing a 'Forgiveness Letter' for a past or current conflict? What do you think this exercise could bring to your emotional landscape? Would it be a bridge to closure, or a first step on the path to reconciliation?

Chapter 7 Wrap-Up: Transforming Conflict into Connection Through Apology and Forgiveness

As we reach the end of this exploration into the alchemy of apology, let's take a moment to reflect on the transformative journey we've embarked upon. We've delved into the complexities of genuine apologies, navigated the psychological labyrinth of forgiveness, and even penned hypothetical "Forgiveness Letters." But the real value of these insights lies not in their conceptual richness, but in their real-world application.

We started this chapter with the metaphor of alchemy—a mysterious process of transformation—and it's worth returning to that imagery as we conclude. Just as alchemists sought to transmute base metals into gold, mastering the art of apology and forgiveness has the potential to transform the base emotions of resentment, anger, and guilt into the golden qualities of understanding, empathy, and love.

However, remember that the true alchemy doesn't happen in isolation; it happens in the crucible of human relationships. It's in those moments of raw vulnerability, where you offer or accept a genuine apology, that a new element is forged—one that strengthens the bonds of your relationships and enriches your emotional well-being.

So, as you close this chapter, consider this: What raw materials do you have in your life right now that could benefit from the alchemy of apology? Are there fractured relationships that could be mended, or emotional wounds that could be healed? Most importantly, are you willing to step into the alchemist's lab of your own life to find out?

The toolkit of skills you've gained here is not meant to gather dust on a theoretical shelf. It's designed to be used, experimented with, and refined through real conversations and emotional exchanges. So, shall we agree to meet in the lab—the real world—and put these transformative insights to the test?

Pit Stop for Reflection: Think Like an Alchemist

As we close this chapter on the transformative power of apology and forgiveness, let's pause for a moment of introspection. These reflection points serve as your personal pit stop—a place to refuel your understanding and sharpen your awareness before you continue on this journey.

1. The Genuine Apology: Can you remember a time when you received an apology that felt truly genuine? What elements made it feel sincere and how did that experience differ from receiving a less authentic apology?

2. Barriers to Apologizing: What obstacles or fears do you encounter when you're the one who needs to offer an apology? Is it a fear of vulnerability, or perhaps a reluctance to admit wrongdoing?

3. Forgiveness as Liberation: Reflect on a moment when you forgave someone. How did it feel? Did you experience it as a form of self-liberation, as if a weight had been lifted?

4. The Power of Writing: Considering the "Forgiveness Letter" exercise, do you think putting your feelings into words could help you either grant or seek forgiveness more effectively? Why or why not?

5. The Alchemist's Lab: As you move forward, what specific situations or relationships in your life could benefit from the "alchemy" of apology and forgiveness? What steps are you willing to take to initiate this transformation?

Take your time with these questions. You might even want to jot down your thoughts in a journal. The act of writing can deepen your insights, helping you integrate the lessons of this chapter into your daily life.

Remember, the journey toward mastering the art of apology and forgiveness is not a sprint; it's more like a pilgrimage. Each step, each insight, brings you closer to becoming a more compassionate and understanding individual. So, are you ready to take the next step?

Chapter 8: Navigating Complex Scenarios

"Adaptability is about the powerful difference between adapting to cope and adapting to win."

– Max McKeown

Have you ever felt like a skilled sailor in one sea of conversation but a castaway in another? You navigate workplace dialogues with the finesse of a seasoned captain but find yourself shipwrecked in the stormy waters of family discussions. Or perhaps you're a maestro at handling conflicts among friends, but when it comes to professional settings, you feel like you're walking a tightrope without a safety net.

Welcome to Chapter 8: Navigating Complex Scenarios. Consider this chapter your comprehensive field guide—a multifaceted compass that can help you traverse the many landscapes of human interaction. Here, we'll take all the principles, tools, and techniques we've explored so far and adapt them to various settings. From the rigid hierarchies of the workplace to the emotionally charged arenas of family and friendships, we'll examine how the art of constructive conversation can be your North Star.

This chapter aims to show you that while the settings may change, the fundamental approaches to constructive conversation remain constant. Think of it as the utility knife of this book—a tool versatile enough for any circumstance, yet specific enough to make a real difference. Are you ready to discover how to apply these timeless principles in the ever-changing settings of your life?

Let's set sail.

The Workplace: The Boardroom, The Watercooler, and Everywhere In-Between

Ah, the workplace—a melting pot of diverse personalities, roles, and agendas, all confined within cubicles, open spaces, or perhaps Zoom calls. Conversations here can be as varied as the tasks on your to-do list. One minute you're negotiating a project timeline with a superior, and the next, you're navigating the sensitive terrain of team dynamics. So how can the principles of constructive conversations be adapted to such a complex setting?

Conflict Resolution with Colleagues

Imagine this: you're in a team meeting, and a colleague publicly criticizes your approach to a project. Your initial impulse might be to go on the defensive, but remember our journey through empathic listening and the Socratic Method. Instead of launching into a counter-argument, try posing a clarifying question like, "Could you elaborate on what you think could be improved?" This not only demonstrates that you're open to constructive feedback but also shifts the conversation from adversarial to collaborative.

Negotiating with Superiors

The stakes are often higher when conversing with those above you in the company hierarchy. Here, the principles of creating a 'safe space' can be invaluable. Before diving into a negotiation or difficult discussion, consider setting some ground rules. For example, you might suggest, "Could we agree to be open to each other's ideas and address any disagreements respectfully?" This establishes a psychological safety net that can make the subsequent conversation far more fruitful.

The Utility of Apology

Don't underestimate the power of a sincere apology in a professional setting. As we've seen in Chapter 7, a genuine apology can transform conflicts and foster personal growth. If you've made an error, acknowledging it openly not only paves the way for resolution but also enhances your credibility.

The Role of Emotional Intelligence

Remember our exploration of emotional triggers? Being aware of your emotional state and that of your colleagues can offer you a significant advantage in professional settings. It's akin to having a barometer in a ship—forewarning you of emotional storms that could capsize a constructive conversation.

The principles we've discussed so far are not just theoretical musings; they're practical tools that can be adapted to the intricate dynamics of the workplace. By applying these principles, you can transform the office from a battlefield of egos into a forum for productive and respectful dialogue.

So, let's pause for a moment. Can you recall a recent workplace conversation that could have benefited from these principles? How would you apply them in future professional interactions?

Family Dynamics: The Heart and the Hearth

The family setting is often described as a 'safe haven,' but let's be honest—it can also be a battleground of unspoken rules, loaded glances, and emotional landmines. It's a space where conversations have far-reaching implications, sometimes echoing through generations. So, how can the principles we've delved into so far apply to the family setting?

Creating a Safe Space at Home

Imagine it's a Sunday dinner, and a contentious topic comes up. Tensions rise, voices escalate, and suddenly, what should be a pleasant meal turns into a free-for-all argument. This is where the concept of 'Creating a Safe Space' can come into play. Could you, perhaps, intervene and say, "Hey, why don't we all take a deep breath and agree to listen to each other before jumping to conclusions?" Such a simple act can defuse tensions and create an environment where everyone feels heard. Remember, a safe space isn't just a physical location; it's an emotional and psychological state that fosters constructive conversations.

The Socratic Method: Not Just for Philosophers

The Socratic Method might sound lofty for a family setting, but its essence—asking probing questions to stimulate critical thinking—can be extremely useful. Suppose your teenager is pushing boundaries, a classic rite of passage. Rather than issuing a flat-out 'no,' try asking, "What do you think could be the consequences of doing this?" This kind of questioning not only encourages them to think but also shows that you respect their ability to reason.

Apologies and Emotional Healing

Family is often where we experience our first conflicts and, consequently, our first apologies. The art of a meaningful apology, complete with acknowledgment and a commitment to making amends, can mend fences and heal old wounds. Remember our discussion about the "Alchemy of Apology"? Its principles are perhaps most potent within the family, where emotional stakes are incredibly high.

The Complexity of Family Hierarchies

Unlike the workplace, family dynamics often don't adhere to a clear hierarchy, making conversations complex and unpredictable. Here, emotional intelligence is your best ally. Being aware of non-verbal cues, emotional states, and potential triggers can help you navigate conversations more skillfully.

Family relationships offer a fertile ground for applying the principles of constructive conversations. Through active listening, genuine apologies, and even philosophical questioning, we can turn fraught family moments into opportunities for deeper understanding and enduring connections.

Pause for reflection: Can you think of a recent family conversation that went awry? How could these principles have turned the tide?

Friendships: The Role of Constructive Conversations

Ah, friendships—the relationships we choose, yet sometimes find as complex as any we're born into. Without the formality of a workplace or the long history of family dynamics, friendships provide a unique arena to exercise the art of constructive conversation.

The Subtleties of Friendship

Friendships often lack the hierarchical structure we find in other relationships, making them feel like safe spaces for open dialogue. But this absence of formality can also lead to a minefield of unspoken expectations and emotional complexities. It's like a jazz ensemble: everyone's got their instrument, there are no strict rules, but oh boy, can it get discordant if someone's out of sync.

The Power of Constructive Conversations

In friendships, the tools we've been honing—active listening, empathic understanding, and skillful questioning—become even more critical. Imagine a friendship as a garden. It requires regular tending, and sometimes that means pulling out the weeds of misunderstandings or planting seeds for deeper connection. Just as you wouldn't use a sledgehammer to plant a delicate seedling, you wouldn't bring a confrontational tone to a conversation with a friend you value.

Navigating the Emotional Landscape

Friendships often carry a heavy emotional investment. When a friend disappoints us or crosses a boundary, it's not just an isolated incident; it's felt as a dent in the emotional bank account that you've both been contributing to. Here, the art of apology and the practice of forgiveness can be transformative. Remember the alchemy of a genuine apology? It has the power to mend the fissures that sometimes develop in friendships.

Adaptation of Tools and Techniques

So, how can the principles we've discussed adapt to friendships? Active listening allows you to really hear your friend's perspective, free from judgment. Creating a safe space can make sensitive conversations less daunting. And the Socratic Method? It's a fantastic tool for challenging assumptions, even in a casual setting. "Why do you feel that way?" can open doors to understanding that a simple "I disagree" would slam shut.

In the realm of friendships, every conversation has the potential to either deepen the relationship or create distance. The choice, often, is in how we converse. The principles in this book offer not just a lifeline for when things get tough, but a manual for nurturing friendships that are deeply fulfilling.

Case Studies and Real-Life Examples

The proof of the pudding, as they say, is in the eating. In other words, all the theories, principles, and techniques we've explored so far are only as good as their real-world applications. Let's dive into some case studies and real-life examples that showcase how these principles can shine in various settings.

Workplace Scenario: Navigating a Team Conflict

The Setup:

Imagine you're Sarah, a project manager in a tech company. You find yourself in the middle of a dispute between Alex, a software developer, and Taylor, a UI/UX designer. Alex feels that Taylor isn't delivering designs on time, affecting the development timeline. Taylor, on the other hand, feels that Alex doesn't appreciate the complexity of the design process.

Step 1: Creating a Safe Space

Before diving into the discussion, you as Sarah set the ground rules. "Let's agree to listen fully before responding and to avoid blaming or accusing. Does that work for everyone?" This sets the tone and creates a psychologically safe environment.

Step 2: Active Listening

Sarah gives each person the floor to express their concerns. While Alex or Taylor speaks, she makes it a point to nod, make eye contact, and occasionally paraphrase to ensure understanding—"So Alex, what I hear you saying is that the delays are affecting other timelines, correct?"

Step 3: Employing the Socratic Method

Instead of directly proposing a solution, Sarah asks open-ended questions aimed at stimulating critical thinking. "Taylor, can you help us understand the challenges you face in the design process? And Alex, have you considered those challenges when setting your expectations?"

Step 4: The Art of Apology and Forgiveness

Once both parties understand each other's challenges better, Sarah encourages them to apologize for any misunderstandings. "Would either of you like to say something?" Alex acknowledges the complexity of Taylor's work, and Taylor apologizes for any communication lapses. It's a step toward mutual forgiveness.

Step 5: Actionable Steps

Finally, Sarah guides them toward creating an action plan. "What steps can we agree on to ensure smoother collaboration in the future?" Both commit to more transparent communication and set new, realistic deadlines.

Through this case study, we see how each element—from setting up a safe space to the fine art of apology—plays a critical role in navigating workplace conflicts. While the setting is professional, the principles of constructive conversation are universal, aren't they?

Family Scenario: Resolving a Generational Gap Conflict

The Setup:

Imagine you're Jamie, a parent of two teenagers, Jordan and Alex. Jordan, the older of the two, is eager to go on a gap year to travel and explore career options. You, on the other hand, are concerned about the delay this will cause in Jordan's education. Tensions are high, and a constructive conversation seems almost impossible.

Step 1: Creating a Safe Space

Before discussing this contentious topic, you establish some ground rules: "Let's agree to listen to each other's point of view, even if we disagree, without interrupting or dismissing the other person." This sets a respectful tone for the dialogue.

Step 2: Active Listening

You start by giving Jordan the floor to express their reasons for wanting a gap year. Instead of immediately countering with your concerns, you listen attentively, nod, and paraphrase for clarity: "So, you feel a gap year would give you the time to explore what really interests you, correct?"

Step 3: Empathy and Validation

You validate Jordan's feelings without necessarily agreeing with the decision: "I can see why the idea of exploring your interests before committing to a career path is appealing to you."

Step 4: The Socratic Method

You engage Jordan in a series of open-ended questions aimed at critical thinking: "Have you considered how the gap year would affect your educational timeline? What's your plan for making the most out of this year?"

Step 5: The Alchemy of Apology

Acknowledging the emotional weight of the situation, you offer a heartfelt apology: "I'm sorry if my initial reaction seemed dismissive of your aspirations. I just worry about your future, as any parent would."

Step 6: Co-creating a Solution

You both agree to research the pros and cons of a gap year and to consult with people who've taken that path. This shared project serves as a commitment to mutual understanding and respect.

This family scenario demonstrates that even in intimate, emotionally charged settings, the principles of constructive conversation can be extraordinarily effective. Remember, whether it's a boardroom or a living room, the objective remains the same: mutual understanding and growth.

Friendship Scenario: Navigating the Rocky Terrain of Unmet Expectations

The Setup:

You're Taylor, and you've been friends with Morgan for over a decade. Recently, you noticed Morgan becoming distant and less communicative. You're concerned but also a bit hurt. When you finally bring it up, Morgan seems defensive, leading to a tense atmosphere.

Step 1: Creating a Safe Space

You choose a neutral setting—a local coffee shop where you've shared many heart-to-hearts before. You open with, "Hey, can we talk? I've noticed we're not as close as we used to be, and I really value our friendship. Can we have an open and honest discussion about it?"

Step 2: Active Listening

Morgan starts talking about feeling overwhelmed with work and family issues. Instead of interjecting with your feelings, you nod and paraphrase: "So, you've been under a lot of stress lately?"

Step 3: Empathy and Validation

You express understanding: "I can see why you'd pull away when dealing with so much. I'm sorry you're going through this."

Step 4: The Socratic Method

Instead of accusing or assuming, you ask open-ended questions: "Have you found that withdrawing helps you manage stress? Is there a way I can support you without adding to your stress?"

Step 5: The Alchemy of Apology

You take a moment to acknowledge any wrongs, "I'm sorry if my approach earlier seemed like I was attacking you. That was not my intent."

Step 6: Words vs. Actions

Morgan apologizes too and suggests a weekly check-in call to maintain the friendship without the pressure of frequent hangouts. You both agree this is a reasonable and actionable step.

The friendship scenario shows that even when there's no formal hierarchy or explicit rules, the pillars of constructive conversation can clear up misunderstandings and mend relationships. Friendships may be casual, but the emotions and expectations are real—making the need for effective communication just as critical.

Chapter 8 Wrap-Up: The Universal Language of Constructive Conversations

As we close this chapter, it's worth pausing to appreciate the incredible versatility of the principles and techniques we've discussed. Whether you're navigating the political intricacies of a workplace, the emotional complexities of family dynamics, or the delicate balances within friendships, the tools in your conversational toolkit remain largely the same.

You see, the art of constructive conversation is akin to a universal language. It's a language that, when spoken fluently, can transcend contexts, break down barriers, and forge connections that are deep and meaningful. And just like any language, it requires regular practice. The case studies we went through are not just hypothetical scenarios but practical exercises in applying this universal language in diverse settings.

So, as we step away from this chapter, remember: the settings may change, but the essence of constructive conversations remains steadfast. Whether you're in the boardroom or at the dinner table, the principles of active listening, empathy, and thoughtful inquiry are your trusty companions.

Pit Stop for Reflection

Here we are, at another pit stop. Take a moment to reflect on your own experiences in various settings—work, family, and friendships. This is where the theories and principles we've discussed truly meet the complexity of real-world situations.

1. Cross-Context Application: Can you think of a specific example in each of these settings—workplace, family, and friendships—where you could have applied the principles in this book? What would you have done differently?
2. Unique Challenges: Are there unique challenges or roadblocks you face in one setting that you haven't encountered in the others? Could it be the formality of the workplace, the emotional intensity of family, or the unspoken expectations in friendships?

3. Most Applicable Tool: Which tool or technique discussed in this chapter do you find most applicable to your own life? Is it the active listening skills for workplace discussions, the art of apology in family settings, or the Socratic questioning in friendships?

4. Learning from Scenarios: Did any of the case studies resonate with you? Have you faced a similar situation, and if so, how did you handle it?

5. Forward-Looking: Looking ahead, how do you envision applying these principles in the future? Are there upcoming situations where you see an opportunity to practice these skills?

Take some time to ponder these questions. They're not just an exercise in introspection but a way to internalize the lessons so that they become second nature. The next time you find yourself in a challenging conversational setting, you'll have this toolbox at your disposal, ready to build bridges instead of walls.

With these reflections, let's prepare ourselves to venture into the next chapter, further equipped to navigate the intricacies of human interactions. Ready?

Chapter 9: The Virtual Frontier

"In the digital age, all human experience is one click away. So is all misunderstanding."

– Esther Perel

In a world increasingly governed by screens and algorithms, we find ourselves navigating a new kind of wilderness—the virtual frontier. Think of this as the 21st-century equivalent of the Wild West, where the promise of connection and discovery coexists with the potential for missteps and conflicts. This frontier is not forged by wagons and railways but by fiber-optic cables and Wi-Fi signals. The stakes are different, but the need for constructive conversations remains just as critical, if not more so.

Why, you ask? The absence of physical proximity in online interactions can either be a liberating force or a recipe for disaster. The computer screen can serve as both a window and a shield, enabling us to reach across the globe or hide behind anonymity. It's a duality that carries its own set of rules, challenges, and opportunities.

This chapter aims to be your guidebook for navigating these digital landscapes. How do you maintain the art of constructive conversation when stripped of non-verbal cues and the nuances that face-to-face interaction affords? How do you manage the pace of a discussion that can escalate from zero to a hundred in the span of a few clicks? Just as importantly, how can you bring empathy into a realm where emotions are often reduced to emojis?

If you've ever found yourself tangled in the web of an online argument or regretted hitting 'send' too soon, this chapter is for you. It's a guide to being as thoughtful, empathic, and effective online as you would hope to be in person. So grab your metaphorical compass and canteen; we're about to explore the virtual frontier.

Unique Challenges of Online Conversations and Conflicts

Navigating online conversations is akin to playing a game of chess in the dark. You know the rules, you have your strategy, but you can't see your opponent's face or read their body language. This absence of non-verbal cues is a major hurdle in digital dialogue. In a face-to-face interaction, a raised eyebrow or a subtle nod can add layers of meaning, helping us interpret what's being said. Online, we're left to guess the tone and intention behind plain text, which can easily lead to misinterpretation.

And then there's what some call "keyboard courage"—the audacity we sometimes feel when separated by a screen. Have you ever found yourself typing out a response online that you would never say in a face-to-face interaction? It's as if the screen grants us a strange form of bravery, allowing us to throw caution—and sometimes decency—to the wind. This can escalate conflicts at an alarming rate, turning what could have been a constructive conversation into a combative exchange.

But why does this happen? Part of it could be attributed to the 'disinhibition effect,' a psychological phenomenon where the lack of face-to-face accountability makes us behave more impulsively. It's like being in a car, somewhat anonymous, and feeling freer to honk at someone; except, in the virtual world, we're not just honking, we're often shouting.

So how do we bring the same level of care, nuance, and respect to online conversations that we aim for in person? Recognizing these unique challenges is the first step. Being aware of the limitations and pitfalls of digital dialogue can arm us with the mindfulness needed to navigate it effectively. Think of it as understanding the terrain of this new frontier—a necessary step before we can venture further into its vast landscapes.

The Speed Factor: The Rapid-Fire Nature of Digital Communication

Imagine a snowball rolling down a hill, gathering mass and momentum as it descends. That's how quickly an online conversation can escalate into a full-blown conflict. One minute, you're engaged in what seems like a civil discussion; the next, you're caught in a whirlwind of rapid-fire responses, each more heated than the last. Ever been there?

So what fuels this acceleration? It's the immediacy of digital platforms. In face-to-face interactions, pauses are natural. There's time to think, reflect, even take a sip of your coffee as you compose your thoughts.

But online, the pace is dictated by how fast you can type, often incentivized by real-time "read" and "typing" indicators that make us feel compelled to respond swiftly. This quick tempo leaves little room for reflection, making it all too easy to shoot from the hip rather than the brain.

And let's not forget the role that the endless stream of notifications play in this speed factor. Each ping is a potential catalyst for conflict, urging us to respond before we've even had the chance to fully digest what's been said. It's like playing a high-stakes game of ping-pong where the ball is always in your court, demanding immediate action.

The result? Words are fired off without forethought, the conversation escalates, and before you know it, both parties are entrenched in their positions, armed with hastily typed responses that serve to inflame rather than illuminate. The snowball has become an avalanche, and digging yourself out becomes an exhausting, often futile, endeavor.

So, the next time you find yourself in an online debate, perhaps it's worth asking: Is this rapid-fire pace serving the conversation, or is it derailing it? Could slowing down be the key to elevating the dialogue?

Anonymity and Accountability: The Double-Edged Sword of Digital Cloaks

Ah, the intoxicating allure of anonymity—the digital mask that emboldens some to say things they'd never dare utter in person. Have you ever encountered an online 'troll'? Someone who spews negativity, safe in the knowledge that they are shielded by a username and perhaps even a cartoon avatar? It's a phenomenon that's become all too common in our digital age.

You see, anonymity can be both a gift and a curse. On one hand, it allows for freedom of expression, enabling people to share opinions or seek advice without fear of real-world repercussions. But on the other, it can severely dilute the sense of accountability that usually governs human interactions. When your actions are disconnected from your identity, the social and ethical guidelines that typically guide your behavior can become blurred.

Think of it like driving a car with tinted windows. You're less visible to other drivers, which might make you feel more secure or private. But if you're not careful, that same sense of invisibility can lead to irresponsible driving—cutting people off, speeding, or worse. Online, this manifests as the infamous "keyboard courage"—the audacity to be confrontational, judgmental, or outright cruel, simply because you're hidden behind a screen.

The absence of real-world consequences creates a moral gray area. It shifts the balance between ego and empathy, often allowing the former to overpower the latter. And when ego takes the wheel, constructive conversation takes a backseat, locked away in the trunk along with respect and understanding.

So, how do we navigate this complex landscape? It starts with self-awareness. Even if you're anonymous, you're still you. Your words, whether typed or spoken, have an impact. It's vital to bring the same level of integrity to online conversations as you would to those face-to-face. Because in the end, the mask of anonymity is just that—a mask. And masks can be taken off, revealing the person behind them.

Have you ever been tempted to behave differently online because of the shield of anonymity? What stopped you, or what did you learn if you gave in to that temptation?

Tips for Digital-Age Constructive Conversations

Tone, the unsung hero of constructive conversations. In face-to-face interactions, tone is the melodious undercurrent that brings color to our words. But what happens when you strip away the vocal inflections, the facial expressions, and the body language? You're left with mere text on a screen, susceptible to the pitfalls of misinterpretation. Have you ever sent a text, only to have the recipient completely misunderstand your intentions? It happens more often than we'd like to admit.

So, how do we infuse tone into our digital dialogues? A simple way to start is with emojis. Think of emojis as the "seasoning" in the dish of digital communication. Just as a dash of salt can bring out flavors, a well-placed emoji can lend emotional context to your words. A smiling face can add warmth, while a thumbs-up can convey agreement or support. But remember, less is more; overuse can dilute the message and even come off as unprofessional or insincere.

Clear language is another powerful tool. Ambiguity is the enemy of effective online communication. Instead of saying, "I guess that's okay," which could be read in several ways, opt for unequivocal expressions like, "I

119

totally agree with you," or, "I support that idea." Being explicit leaves less room for misunderstanding.

Another tip? Punctuation. A period at the end of a sentence can make a statement feel final, even abrupt. Exclamation marks can add enthusiasm but can also be read as shouting if overused. Question marks invite responses and can soften a statement into a more collaborative query.

Lastly, there's the option of stepping out of the digital format to clarify tone. If a conversation seems to be spiraling into misunderstanding, a quick voice note or phone call can do wonders to clear the air.

Think about a recent text conversation you had. Was the tone clear? Were there moments of confusion that could have been avoided with better tone management? What will you do differently next time?

The Pause Button: The Digital Art of Holding Your Tongue

The allure of instant messaging—the ability to fire off a message at lightning speed. But, have you ever stopped to consider the double-edged sword that is the 'send' button? Quick responses might be convenient, but they can also lead to rapid-fire exchanges that escalate conflicts almost instantaneously. Ever found yourself typing so fast during an online debate that your fingers could barely keep up with your thoughts? It's a common experience, but one that often doesn't end well.

So, here's where the "Pause Button" comes into play. Just like taking a deep breath in a face-to-face confrontation, pausing before responding online offers you a moment of reflection. How long should this pause be? It depends on the situation. Sometimes, a few seconds are enough to reevaluate your message; other times, stepping away for a few minutes—or even hours—can bring clarity.

The pause serves multiple purposes. First, it allows you to assess the tone and content of your message critically. Are you being respectful? Is your message clear? Second, it provides a buffer against impulsivity. In the heat of the moment, we often say things we later regret. A pause can serve as a safeguard against such slip-ups.

Third, the pause can also serve as a cooling-off period. When emotions are running high, our rational thinking often takes a backseat. A brief pause can help you regain your emotional equilibrium, making room for more constructive dialogue.

It's a simple tactic, but one that requires conscious effort to implement. Just like in mindfulness practices, the pause creates a gap between stimulus and response, giving you the opportunity to choose your actions rather than react impulsively.

Reflect on this: Can you recall an online conversation where a pause would have made all the difference? How will you implement this tool in your future digital interactions?

Virtual Empathy: The Heartbeat in a Digital World

In face-to-face conversations, empathy often flows naturally through gestures, facial expressions, and tone of voice. Online, however, these non-verbal cues are absent, making the expression of empathy a bit of a high-wire act. How do we maintain that human touch in an environment made up of pixels and text?

For starters, choose your words carefully. Simple yet potent phrases like "I understand where you're coming from," "That must be hard for you," or "I can see why you would feel that way" can go a long way in acknowledging someone else's perspective or emotional state. Remember, empathy isn't about agreeing; it's about understanding.

Another useful approach is to validate before you debate. For example, if someone shares an opinion you disagree with, try acknowledging their viewpoint first. You could say, "I see what you're saying about [X]. Have you considered [Y]?" This makes the other person feel heard, which often lowers defensive walls and paves the way for a more constructive exchange.

Sometimes, online platforms offer unique tools to convey empathy. For instance, the appropriate use of emojis can serve as digital stand-ins for facial expressions. A heart emoji or a smiley face can sometimes communicate warmth and understanding more succinctly than words. However, be cautious. Emojis can also be easily misunderstood or come off as unprofessional in certain contexts.

Lastly, if you find that a text-based conversation is becoming too heated or complicated, suggest switching to a more personal form of communication. A voice or video call can reintroduce the missing elements of tone and expression, making empathy easier to convey and perceive.

So, when was the last time you felt truly understood in an online conversation? How did that make you feel? And moving forward, how will you channel that experience into expressing virtual empathy yourself?

The "Zoom Rule": Humanizing Digital Interactions

Ever found yourself in a tense back-and-forth exchange of text messages or emails that seemed to be getting nowhere? It's like a digital tug-of-war, where each side is pulling but nobody's winning. This is where the "Zoom Rule" comes in handy. The rule is simple yet transformative: When a text-based conversation starts spiraling into conflict, switch to video chat or a phone call.

Why is this effective? Imagine you're trying to solve a puzzle with half of the pieces missing. That's what arguing through text is like. You lack the nuances—the tone of voice, the facial expressions, the pauses—that fill in the emotional gaps. A video or voice call adds those missing pieces back into the equation, making it easier to understand each other's emotional state and intentions.

Switching to a more "human" mode of communication can also break the cycle of impulsivity that often fuels online arguments. It's much harder to hit "send" on a scathing message when you have to say it directly to someone's face. Video calls force us to confront the human being on the other side of the screen, reminding us that behind every username and profile picture is a person with feelings, just like us.

Still, the "Zoom Rule" isn't about avoiding difficult conversations; it's about enriching them. When you switch to a more direct form of communication, you're not retreating—you're advancing the conversation to a place where real understanding can occur.

So, consider this: Are there recent conflicts you've had online that could have benefited from the "Zoom Rule"? How would the dynamics have changed if you could see the other person's face or hear their voice? And how might you implement this rule in your future digital interactions to elevate them from destructive to constructive?

Wrapping Up: Mastering the Digital Frontier

So there we have it—the wilderness of online conversations isn't so untamed after all. It has its own rules, its own challenges, but also its own unique opportunities for constructive engagement. The key takeaway? The principles of effective, empathetic communication are not confined to any single setting. They are as applicable in the boundless landscape of digital interaction as they are in a cozy living room chat.

Navigating the virtual frontier skillfully is about adapting, not abandoning, the principles we've discussed throughout this journey. It's about recognizing that while the setting may change, the core elements—empathy, active listening, constructive questioning—remain constant.

In this digital age, our 'conversational sphere' has expanded beyond physical boundaries. Let's ensure that our commitment to constructive conversations does the same. After all, the screen and keyboard are not barriers but bridges, capable of connecting us in ways that enrich, rather than diminish, our shared human experience.

As you log off from this chapter, consider this: The internet doesn't have to be a battleground; it can be a meeting ground. And with the tools you've now acquired, you're well-equipped to make it so.

Pit Stop for Reflection

1. Online Conflicts: Have you ever found yourself embroiled in an online conflict that spiraled out of control? If so, what elements do you think contributed to that escalation? Was it the anonymity, the speed, or perhaps a lack of tonal cues?

2. Applying Principles: How can you apply the principles of constructive conversation in a digital setting? Can you think of a recent online interaction where the "Pause Button" or "Zoom Rule" could have made a difference?

3. Tone and Empathy: Have you ever misinterpreted someone's tone in a text-based conversation? How did it impact the dialogue? Going forward, how might you convey empathy or tone more effectively online?

4. Accountability: How does the cloak of digital anonymity affect your own behavior in online discussions? Are you more bold, confrontational, or perhaps even more honest than you would be face-to-face?

5. Future Steps: Given what you've learned, what are some actionable steps you can take to ensure your online conversations are as

constructive as your in-person ones? Think about specific strategies like setting a timer before responding, using video calls for heated discussions, or employing emojis to clarify your tone.

This pit stop is an invitation to apply your newfound understanding in real-time, digital settings. As you reflect, you're not just a passive consumer of information; you're becoming an active, empowered participant in any conversation—virtual or otherwise—that you engage in. So, are you ready to take these insights online?

Interlude: Stories of Transformation

In the chapters that have unfolded so far, we've looked into the theory and mechanics of constructive conversations. We've dissected the elements that can turn a simple dialogue into an opportunity for growth, connection, and resolution. But what happens when these principles escape the pages of a book and come to life in the real world? That's what this Interlude is all about.

The purpose of this section is twofold. First, it serves as a source of inspiration, demonstrating that the principles we've explored aren't just abstract concepts but actionable strategies that people have successfully applied in their lives. Second, it validates your journey as a reader, affirming that yes, these ideas do work and they can transform how you communicate, resolve conflicts, and connect with others.

Why do stories matter? Because they tap into something deeply ingrained in the human psyche. Stories don't just entertain; they educate, inspire, and foster empathy. They serve as both a mirror and a window—reflecting your own experiences while also offering a glimpse into someone else's world. In sharing these real-life narratives, we aim to bridge the gap between theory and practice, providing you not just with knowledge, but with hope.

So, sit back and immerse yourself in these stories of transformation. Let them serve as beacons, guiding you through your own journey toward more constructive and meaningful conversations.

Collection of Real-Life Stories and Testimonials

Workplace Transformation: A Case of Unspoken Tensions

Let me share the story of Emily, a middle-level manager at a tech company. Emily found herself in a constant state of tension with Alex, a team member who was extremely competent but also somewhat abrasive. Their interactions were like trying to mix oil and water—impossible. Emily considered confronting Alex but worried that a direct approach could lead to an argument, further fracturing their already strained relationship.

After reading about the importance of creating a "safe space" for dialogue, Emily decided to apply the principles. She invited Alex for a one-on-one meeting, away from the hustle and bustle of the office. Emily set the stage by laying down some ground rules. "Let's both agree to listen first and speak second, and to give each other the benefit of the doubt," she suggested.

Emily employed active listening techniques, paraphrasing what Alex said to ensure she understood his point of view. She then used the Socratic Method to question some of Alex's assumptions gently. "Can you help me understand why you think this approach is the best?" she'd ask, allowing Alex to expound on his reasoning rather than getting defensive.

Most importantly, Emily did something she had never done before: she showed vulnerability. She shared her concerns about the team's dynamics openly, admitting that she too could be part of the problem.

The result? Alex started to let his guard down. He admitted that he sometimes pushed too hard because he felt pressure to perform. By the end of the meeting, both agreed on actionable steps to improve their working relationship, including regular check-ins and clearer communication protocols.

Emily later wrote in a testimonial, "The strategies I learned helped me not only resolve a critical workplace conflict but also gave me tools to foster a culture of open dialogue within my team."

This real-life example illustrates the immense power of constructive conversation. Emily didn't just solve a problem; she transformed a relationship. And she did it by applying the very principles we've explored together in this book.

Family Reconciliation: The Thanksgiving Truce

Picture this: Sarah and her brother Tom hadn't spoken in two years due to a family dispute over their late father's will. Every holiday since had been a tense affair, with family members walking on eggshells, fearing an eruption of old grievances. Sarah felt the distance growing, and the family seemed to be splitting at the seams.

After engaging with the idea of "The Alchemy of Apology," Sarah knew something had to change. But how do you approach such a loaded topic, laden with years of emotional baggage? Sarah took to heart the notion of the "Four Rs"—Recognition, Responsibility, Remorse, and Repair—as a framework for her apology.

At the next Thanksgiving dinner, she seized a private moment with Tom and initiated a difficult yet overdue conversation. "Tom, can we talk?" she started. "I've had some time to think, and I recognize that my actions during the dispute about Dad's will hurt you. I take full responsibility for that."

Then came the remorse: "I'm truly sorry for any pain I've caused." And finally, the repair: "I'm committed to making things right between us. Can we find a way to move forward?"

Sarah was keenly aware of the importance of timing and setting, choosing a moment when they were both mentally prepared for a deep conversation. She also followed the advice of creating a safe space, setting ground rules for the conversation that included active listening and no interruptions.

Tom was taken aback at first but then reciprocated with his own set of grievances and apologies. The conversation wasn't easy—far from it—but it was honest, direct, and heartfelt. By the end of it, both had tears in their eyes, not just from the weight of their past conflicts but also from the newfound hope for a reconciled future.

In the months that followed, Sarah and Tom started rebuilding their relationship. They began to spend time together outside of obligatory family events, and other family members noticed the shift in dynamics. The tension that once loomed over family gatherings began to dissipate, replaced by a newfound warmth.

Sarah later reflected, "That one conversation didn't fix everything, but it was a start—a significant one. The principles of constructive conversation gave us the roadmap to navigate an emotional minefield and come out on the other side, not unscathed, but certainly united."

Sarah's story showcases the transformative power of applying these principles in a family setting. She not only mended her relationship with her brother but also altered the dynamics of her entire family.

Does Sarah's story echo challenges you've faced? How might her approach inspire you in your own life?

Friendship Renewed: The Long-Lost Connection

Let's turn our attention to Aaliyah and Laura, best friends since their freshman year of college. They had been through thick and thin, breakups and graduations, moves, and career changes. But over the years, life happened. They both got caught up in their respective worlds—Aaliyah with her corporate job and Laura with her growing family. Texts turned infrequent, and calls became rare. A simple misunderstanding over a cancelled reunion led to unspoken hurt feelings, and just like that, their once unbreakable friendship seemed to have hit a snag.

Aaliyah stumbled upon the concept of "Virtual Empathy" from this book and realized that if ever there was a time for applying empathy digitally, this was it. She also remembered the idea of the Socratic Method as a tool to illuminate ideas and thought, "What better way to unearth what went wrong?"

So, Aaliyah mustered the courage and reached out to Laura with a simple text: "Hey Laura, I've been thinking a lot about us lately. Can we talk?" Accompanied by a " 😊 ," she hoped this would set a positive tone.

Laura agreed, and they set a time for a video call—after all, humanizing a digital interaction often leads to quicker resolution, as the "Zoom Rule" suggests. On the call, Aaliyah started with the principle of active listening. "I've noticed we've grown apart, and that cancellation seemed to make it worse. I want to understand what you felt. Would you be willing to share?"

Laura, feeling safe and listened to, opened up about how she felt abandoned and assumed Aaliyah no longer valued their friendship because of her busy corporate life. The absence of non-verbal cues in their digital interactions had let misunderstandings fester.

This was a lightbulb moment for Aaliyah. She employed the art of Socratic questioning to clarify assumptions, asking, "Is it that you felt I was too busy for you?" When Laura nodded, Aaliyah knew it was time for a sincere apology. "I'm genuinely sorry, Laura. My actions—or lack of actions—made you feel that way, and I want to make amends."

Aaliyah went a step further by proposing a regular monthly catch-up, demonstrating a commitment to change—a crucial element of making an impactful apology. The result? A friendship on the mend, one virtual conversation at a time.

In Aaliyah and Laura's story, we see how the concepts of virtual empathy, active listening, and the Socratic Method can come together to rescue a friendship on the brink. Not only did they salvage their friendship, but they also learned valuable skills that will help them navigate future bumps in the road.

So, what do you think? Could Aaliyah and Laura's story offer clues for mending a friendship in your own life? How might you implement these principles the next time you find yourself at a crossroads in a friendship?

Digital Peace: The Twitter Feud Turned Collaboration

Meet Marcus and Naomi, two passionate activists in the realm of environmental conservation. Despite sharing the same mission, they found themselves in a heated Twitter dispute over the best approach to tackle climate change. Marcus advocated for policy reform, while Naomi was all about grassroots activism. Their exchange escalated quickly, retweets and quote-tweets amplifying their disagreement to hundreds of followers.

Marcus stumbled upon the concept of the "Pause Button" in this book and realized how applicable it was in this context. Instead of firing back another tweet in the heat of the moment, he took a step back. Marcus paused and asked himself, "What am I really trying to achieve here? Is this Twitter spat helping or hurting the cause we both care about?"

After some reflection, Marcus decided to switch gears. Remembering the "Zoom Rule," he reached out to Naomi via DM and suggested they move the conversation to a more personal setting—a video call. Naomi agreed, intrigued and relieved that Marcus was extending an olive branch.

During the call, Marcus initiated the conversation with active listening and a Socratic approach. He started by saying, "Naomi, I think we both want the same thing: a healthier planet. Can you help me understand why you think grassroots activism is the most effective way to get there?"

Naomi shared her perspective, and because Marcus was genuinely interested in understanding her point of view, she felt heard and respected. This paved the way for a more constructive dialogue. Marcus also shared his views, and they both realized that their approaches were not mutually exclusive; in fact, they could be complementary.

Inspired, they decided to collaborate on a joint campaign that combined policy advocacy with grassroots mobilization. Their Twitter feeds transformed from battlegrounds to platforms for promoting their collaborative project.

So, Marcus and Naomi's story teaches us that even in the rapid-fire, impersonal realm of social media, the principles of constructive conversation can turn conflicts into opportunities for connection and collaboration. It illustrates how the "Pause Button" can give us the space to reassess, and how switching platforms can entirely shift the dynamics of a conversation.

What about you? Have you ever found yourself in a digital conflict that seemed impossible to resolve? Could the tactics Marcus and Naomi employed help you turn a similar situation around?

The Power of Apology: The Reunion of Old Friends

Let's journey into the lives of Mattie and Debbie, two childhood friends who had a falling out during their college years. A misunderstanding led to hurtful words, and before they knew it, years had gone by without any communication. Both held onto resentment but also a sense of loss for a friendship that once meant the world to them.

Debbie stumbled upon this book and was particularly struck by the chapter on "The Alchemy of Apology." The Four Rs—Recognition, Responsibility, Remorse, and Repair—resonated with her. She recognized the weight of her words from years ago, took responsibility for the hurt she had caused, felt genuine remorse, and now wanted to make repairs.

She decided to write Mattie a letter, applying the "Forgiveness Letter" exercise. In the letter, Debbie acknowledged her wrongdoing, expressed her deep remorse, and committed to being a better friend moving forward. She didn't expect anything in return; she simply wanted Mattie to know she was sorry.

Mattie received the letter and was moved to tears. Debbie's heartfelt apology acted like a key, unlocking a door Mattie had shut tightly. She felt seen, heard, and validated. It was as if the apology had given her permission to heal, to let go of the resentment that she didn't even realize was weighing her down.

Feeling the weight lifted, Mattie reached out to Debbie, and they decided to meet. Their reunion was emotional, and Debbie's genuine apology set the tone for a new chapter in their friendship. They couldn't reclaim the lost years, but the power of the apology had given them a chance for many more years of friendship ahead.

The story of Mattie and Debbie serves as a poignant reminder that apologies have a transformative power that can mend broken relationships and heal emotional wounds. It shows how the Four Rs can be a roadmap to reconciliation, and how one act of genuine remorse can change the course of a relationship forever.

How about you? Is there a fractured relationship in your life that could benefit from the healing power of a genuine apology? What would it take for you to take that courageous first step?

Chapter 10: The Journey from Conflict to Connection

*"The most important things to say are those which often
I did not think necessary for me to say—because they were too
obvious."*

– André Gide

We began our exploration with the psychological underpinnings of conflict. It's almost like we put conflict itself on the therapist's couch, examining its various triggers, emotional drivers, and the cognitive biases that often fan its flames. We dissected the inner workings of the human mind, understanding how ingrained patterns of thinking and emotional triggers can turn even a benign situation into a full-blown dispute. Can you recall the role of the amygdala, that small but mighty part of the brain, in our fight-or-flight response? Understanding this was like having a backstage pass to the theater of human reaction.

From the mind, we moved on to the realm of dialogue—the spoken and unspoken exchanges that either deepen conflicts or resolve them. We looked at how the quality of our conversations is often the key to unlocking the puzzle of conflict. Techniques like active listening and open-ended questioning became our navigational tools. We explored the stages of a conversation, from initiation to escalation, and then to either resolution or rupture. How impactful was it to learn about the 'safe space'? That metaphorical room where judgments are suspended, and authentic dialogue can happen. It felt like learning the rules of a new game, didn't it?

And speaking of game-changers, who could forget our deep dive into the Socratic Method? This ancient tool showed us how questioning can be a form of enlightenment. It provided a structured way to challenge assumptions, clarify viewpoints, and ultimately, arrive at a deeper

132

understanding of not just the issue at hand, but also of each other. The Socratic Method was like the Swiss Army knife in our toolkit of constructive conversation, a multi-purpose tool that can be employed in almost any setting, from family dinners to corporate boardrooms.

This road, with its twists and turns, brought us to a clearer understanding of how conflicts originate, how they escalate, and most importantly, how they can be resolved. It equipped us with a new lens through which to view our interactions, a lens that can transform the ordinary into the extraordinary.

The Core Principles: The Pillars of Our Journey

As we transition from reflecting on the path we've tread to peering into the horizon ahead, it's essential to remind ourselves of the core principles that have acted as our compass. These are the ideas and techniques that underpin every lesson we've explored and every transformation we've aspired to.

Constructive Conversation: The Art of Dialogue

We've examined how constructive conversation is not merely about talking but about crafting a shared narrative. It's an interactive process where we dig deep to understand and be understood. It's the art of turning a monologue into a dialogue, a debate into a conversation. This principle was our cornerstone, wasn't it? It's like being given a new language—one that allows us to express ourselves fully while also being receptive to others.

Empathy: The Bridge Between Souls

Empathy was another cornerstone, serving as the emotional bridge that makes true understanding possible. Empathy isn't just about being nice; it's about stepping into another's shoes, seeing the world from their viewpoint, and validating their feelings without necessarily agreeing with their stance. Remember when we discussed empathy as a two-way street? It's as much about giving as it is about receiving. How has practicing empathy changed your interactions with others?

Active Listening: The Quiet Force

Active listening turned out to be a quiet force in our toolkit. By being present and truly hearing what the other person is saying, we allowed for deeper understanding to take place. It's the art of listening not just to respond but to understand. We learned that sometimes the most powerful thing we can say is nothing at all—just listen. Has this principle been a game-changer in your conversations?

The Transformative Power of Apology

And then, there's the alchemy of apology—the transformative power that can turn rifts into bridges and conflicts into opportunities for growth. An apology, when genuine, is not just a statement but a declaration of intent. It's a promise to do better, to be better. The act of saying "I'm sorry" became, in our journey, an act of grace. It's the key to healing, isn't it?

These principles are more than just theoretical constructs; they are living, breathing practices that we can integrate into our daily lives. Each serves a unique function, yet they all work in synergy, like members of a well-coordinated team.

How have these core principles resonated with you? Which one has had the most impact so far, and why?

The Evolution: A Paradigm Shift in Relationships and Personal Growth

What's particularly remarkable about the journey we've undertaken together is that the principles we've learned and internalized don't just apply to isolated incidents or conflicts. Rather, they have the power to bring about a paradigm shift in how we engage with the world at large—transforming not only our conversations but also our relationships and our very approach to personal growth.

Think about it. When we start to converse constructively, practice empathy, listen actively, and embrace the healing power of apology, we're essentially rewriting the script of our relationships. Suddenly, interactions that used to be fraught with tension become opportunities for deeper connection. Family gatherings that once felt like emotional minefields turn into more harmonious occasions. Friendships grow richer, workplaces become more collaborative, and even online interactions take on a more respectful tone. Can you identify a relationship in your life that has already begun to shift due to these principles?

The impact doesn't stop at relationships; it permeates into our personal growth journey as well. By mastering the art of constructive conversation, we become better communicators, sure, but we also become better thinkers, better empathizers, and better human beings. We learn to handle adversity with grace, confront challenges with insight, and turn conflicts into stepping stones for growth. It's like we've been equipped with a GPS system that not only helps us navigate conflicts but also guides us towards becoming more evolved versions of ourselves. How do you feel you've grown personally since beginning this journey?

The transformative effect can even ripple out beyond the personal sphere. By changing the quality of our individual interactions, we contribute to a more empathetic and understanding community and society. It's as if each constructive conversation is a drop of water, and collectively, we have the power to create an ocean of change. Have you noticed any broader impacts of your new conversational skills yet?

So, in embracing these principles, we're not just solving problems; we're evolving. We're becoming the people who not only know how to turn conflicts into opportunities for connection but also have the skills and mindset to make that a consistent practice in every area of life. This is the evolution we're talking about—the transformation from reactive to proactive, from confrontational to constructive, from isolated to interconnected.

Have you started to see this evolution in yourself? What's one area in your life where you feel these principles could make a significant difference?

Your Call to Action

As we've navigated the varied landscapes of human interaction, from the intimate circles of family and friends to the broader arenas of work and digital spaces, we've equipped you with a valuable toolkit. Think of it as your Swiss Army knife for conversations—multifunctional, adaptable, and always handy. It's a set of tools you can, and should, carry with you wherever you go.

The Professional Toolkit

In the professional sphere, this toolkit can be a game-changer. The next time you find yourself in a tense meeting or a salary negotiation, remember the principles of active listening and the Socratic Method. These aren't just theories; they're practical applications that can tilt the balance in your favor, making you not just an employee but a communicator who commands respect.

The Personal Toolkit

In your personal life, whether it's a spat with a family member or a disagreement with a friend, you now have the resources to handle it constructively. Techniques like creating a safe space and the transformative power of a genuine apology can turn potentially explosive situations into opportunities for deepening relationships. Have you considered which tool you'll reach for first in your next personal conflict?

The Digital Toolkit

Let's not forget the digital realm. In an age where a tweet or a text can escalate into a full-blown argument, your toolkit is essential. You've learned how to express virtual empathy, how to pause before hitting 'send,' and when to switch from texting to a more personal form of communication. Each time you do this, you're setting a new standard for digital discourse.

What you hold in your hands, metaphorically speaking, is a treasure trove of skills and insights that can make you a master communicator in any setting. And the best part? This toolkit is ever-expanding. As you go through life, each new conversation gives you the opportunity to refine your skills, add new tools, and become more adept at turning conflicts into constructive conversations.

So, are you ready to wield this toolkit not just as a set of instruments, but as an extension of your own intentions and values?

The Ripple Effect: Beyond the Pages and Into the World

It's tempting to see the end of this book as the end of our journey, but really, it's just the beginning. The wisdom and techniques we've explored here are not meant to be confined to these pages; they are designed to be

136

lived, practiced, and shared. And here's the magical part: each conversation you transform has the power to create a ripple effect that goes far beyond the two people involved.

Imagine if, after a constructive conversation, you leave someone feeling heard, respected, and valued. Chances are, they'll carry that positive energy into their next interaction, and so on. You've not only made your day better but, indirectly, you've contributed to improving someone else's day as well. Isn't that a win-win scenario you'd love to be part of, day in and day out?

But let's think bigger. Imagine applying these principles in a team meeting, a community gathering, or even an online forum. The ripple effect here can be substantial. A constructive conversation in a professional setting could lead to more empathetic company policies. A fruitful family discussion could set the tone for generations of open dialogue. An online interaction that avoids the pitfalls of animosity could set a precedent for how strangers engage on important issues. Have you thought about where you could initiate this ripple effect first?

And it doesn't stop there. In a world that's increasingly polarized and fraught with conflict, the need for constructive conversations is not just a personal necessity; it's a global imperative. Each respectful dialogue, each empathetic response, contributes to a culture of understanding and peace on a larger scale. It's like casting a stone into a pond—the ripples spread out, affecting more and more people, eventually creating a wave of positive change that could, in time, reach far-flung corners of our interconnected world.

Be the Change: Your Power, Your Responsibility, Your Legacy

Here we are, standing at the threshold of a new beginning—a beginning crafted by you, in the choices you make every day. The power to turn conflicts into meaningful connections doesn't just lie in a book, or in theories and techniques. No, that transformative power lies within you, waiting to be harnessed. And the world, now more than ever, is in dire need of that transformation.

In a world marred by division and discord, where headlines are often dominated by conflicts, the actions of a single individual can feel insignificant. But that's a fallacy. Because it's not the grand gestures that change the world;

it's the myriad small ones, accumulating like droplets in a river that eventually bursts its banks. Each constructive conversation you have is a droplet in that river, a ripple in the pond that extends far beyond what the eye can see.

Think of the people you've been inspired by in your life—the leaders, the innovators, or even a parent or a friend. What made them memorable? Was it their ability to shout the loudest or win the most arguments? Or was it their capacity for empathy, their willingness to listen, and their knack for turning adversarial moments into opportunities for mutual growth?

You can be that person for someone else. You can be the change you wish to see in the world. Starting today, right now, with your next conversation. It's not just an opportunity; it's a responsibility. The legacy you leave behind won't just be in the accomplishments you list but in the connections you've deepened, the conflicts you've transformed, and the hearts you've touched.

So go on, step boldly into your next chapter, armed with the principles and techniques you've gathered here. The world is a tapestry of human connections, and you have the power to weave your thread in a way that enriches not just your life, but the lives of everyone you interact with.

Are you ready to be that catalyst of transformation? Because your journey, astonishing in its potential to effect change, is just beginning.

Here's to you—the peacemaker, the bridge-builder, the change-maker. Let's make the world a better place, one constructive conversation at a time.

So, as you close this book, consider this your call to action: don't just be a passive consumer of these principles; be an active agent of change. Initiate the ripple effect. Make it your mission to turn every conversation, no matter how trivial or heated, into an opportunity for connection and growth. After all, if not you, then who? And if not now, then when?

Are you ready to be the catalyst for this ripple effect of positive change?

About the Author: David N. Johnson

David N. Johnson is your everyday individual, not a celebrity, billionaire, or renowned guru, but someone who resonates with the common person—because he is one. For a long time, David believed the myth that one person was too insignificant to make a difference. He thought that impactful change was the responsibility of someone else, someone more qualified.

However, like many, David realized that waiting for change to happen wasn't enough. He understood that it only takes one individual to ignite a spark of transformation. That individual, he argues, is you.

Before setting out to influence others, David believes in the principle of "putting your own oxygen mask on first." He emphasizes the importance of personal growth as a precursor to making a positive impact on others. Through his writings, he explores a range of topics including morality, mindset, altruism, and the pathways to success.

David invites you to engage with his work, share what resonates, and join him on this journey of making a meaningful difference, one step at a time.

He can be found at DavidNJohnson.com

Made in the USA
Monee, IL
12 November 2025

34449555R00079